A WALK ACROSS MICHIGAN

A WALK *Across* MICHIGAN

*Hiking the Michigan
Shore-to-Shore
and Hiking Trail*

WILL SWARTZ

A Walk Across Michigan by Will Swartz

© 2015 by Will Swartz. All rights reserved.

No part of this book may be reproduced in any written, electronic, recording, or photocopying without written permission of the publisher or author. The exception would be in the case of brief quotations embodied in the critical articles or reviews and pages where permission is specifically granted by the publisher or author.

Although every precaution has been taken to verify the accuracy of the information contained herein, the author and publisher assume no responsibility for any errors or omissions. No liability is assumed for damages that may result from the use of information contained within.

Calibri, Cambria and Garamond fonts used with permission from Microsoft.

Calvin & Hobbes cartoon reprinted with permission of Universal UClick. All rights reserved.

Books may be purchased by contacting the publisher and author at:

Will@willswartz.com

Cover Design: Daisy Designs/Anna Holtman

Publisher: Will Swartz Enterprises

Editor: Phillip T. Hopersberger

Library of Congress Control Number: 2015915008

ISBN: 978-0-9967932-7-8

1) Michigan Shore-to-Shore Riding and Hiking Trail–Description and travel

2) Travel–Hiking–Michigan Shore-to-Shore Riding and Hiking Trail

3) Swartz, Will–Travel–Backpacking

First Edition Printed in USA

Bonus Page

Additional photos and resources from **A Walk Across Michigan** can be viewed at the website for this book:

Awalkacrossmichigan.com

I hope they add to your enjoyment of the book.

Are you planning to ride or hike the Michigan Shore-to-Shore Riding and Hiking Trail?
Visit the **STS Trail Website** at:

Michiganshoretoshoretrail.com

For more information about my latest adventures and my other books, visit my website at:

Willswartz.com

FREE BOOK OFFER!
Go to:

Awalkacrossmichigan.com/freebook

To Kate.

My wife, my sherpa and fellow traveler on
The Journey Home.

Acknowledgements

I've used up favors and good will at an alarming rate over the past year. Asking complete strangers for help with a project that they may have little or no interest in - and certainly not much to gain from - requires people who have a generous spirit and I'd like to take this opportunity to express my gratitude for their help and cooperation.

Two professional organizations have had a part in this book. The Michigan Trail Riders Association (MTRA) is the backbone of the Shore-to-Shore Trail. Their unselfish labor to improve, protect and maintain the trail deserves more recognition and praise than they receive. I am grateful for the many hours that members spent with me to share their stories and knowledge of the trail. Chris Rayner, MTRA secretary/treasurer (and also a librarian!) graciously introduced me to many people in the organization and helped in numerous ways. Sally Seaver and Rex LaLonde spent a day of their lives patiently answering my many questions about the trail. Their 50+ crossings were an invaluable source of information. Although I am a man without a horse, I have felt welcomed by their organization.

Librarians rock. I'm thankful to the many members of Michigan Association for Media in Education (MAME) who have supported and encouraged me in this project. Several are part of Team Will and gave me much appreciated feedback in the early stages of writing that helped with the direction this book took. In addition, there is nothing more valuable than a network of librarians to help launch a new book!

Knowlton's Ice Museum, in Port Huron, MI, is a treasure trove of artifacts and information on the ice trade. Director Melissa Davis gave me a personal tour, answered numerous questions and provided the resources to further research this fascinating part of history.

Amanda Holmes, Executive Director at Fishtown Preservation Society, provided materials about Fishtown.

Kim Kelderhouse at the Leland Historical Society was an immense help in locating material on Leelanau and the ice trade. She graciously gave me access to the archives and directed me to resources.

The support team at Kodiak Cameras needs to be given a raise. Their response time to my requests for photo permission and followup were awesome. They get credit for the photo of the River Deer on the cover that was captured with a Comanche Outfitters' Kodiak Series Wi-Fi Trail Camera.

Daisy, of DaisyDesigns, gave me several possible cover concepts and provided the original cover design that was modified by Anna Holtman. Daisy also created the paperback cover and other graphics for me. I highly recommend both Anna and Daisy if you need graphic design work.

Several people have been instrumental in helping me learn about the self publishing industry and book marketing. Jim Cockrum's and Jason Mile's course, *Proven Self Publishing Course*, was invaluable education from authors who have self published books themselves and have a gift for teaching others. In addition, Jason offered personal help by SKYPE and gave me excellent advice.

Udemy courses by Nick Loper (Kindle Launch Plan: $1,400 in 30 Days and an Amazon Bestseller), and Tom Corson-Knowle's (How To Become a Bestselling Author on Amazon), are great introductions to self-publishing.

Ken Filar is a fellow hiker who found my site buried on the Internet and connected to share his knowledge of the trail. He recently completed his own Shore-to-Shore hike and has graciously provided detailed information to use for the companion book to this one, *Hiking the Michigan Shore-to-Shore Riding and Hiking Trail: A Section by Section Guide*.

In the early stages of writing this book I put out a request for volunteers to read my half-baked book and provide feedback. Surprisingly, 60+ people stepped forward and joined Team Will. They provided a wealth of insight and many were willing to help with launching this book by graciously sharing it in their networks and on their social platforms. I'm grateful for their help.

Beverly Edmonds read the entire manuscript and helped with numerous details that helped make this a better book.

Liz Jones, a fellow classmate from Big Rapids High School, proofread and corrected the entire manuscript. Mrs. Kaufman, our former English teacher, would be proud of the grammarian she has become.

Phil Hopesberger is an old friend I reconnected with, who just happens to be a published author/screenwriter/editor. He agreed to take me on as a client and his insight into what was missing from my original manuscript and his creative suggestions are to blame for many of the improvements in this book.

I was thankful for family and friends who came along on various sections of the trail. My brother-in-law Kevin and sons Josh, Caleb and Levi, came along for two days and are great companions to have on the trail and in camp. They are truly a bonus for marrying Kate.

All but one of my five children (Noah, who lives in Texas) were able to hike a section of the trail with me. My daughter,

Noelle, slopped through the mud for a couple of hours with me during a steady downpour and was indignant when her brothers and sister didn't have to face anything even approaching inclement weather during their sections. Jeremy and Josiah are always great fun and made the middle of my hike more than tolerable by adding some much needed camaraderie. Jennifer, spent a glorious morning pacing me to the start of my solo hike.

My brothers Brian and Scott left families and responsibilities at home to come and spend a weekend with their older brother on another of his wild adventures. I treasure the bond we have as brothers. They are always the source of great times and not a few stories! I have no doubt that our brother Dale would have joined this adventure and made the time even better. We miss him greatly.

I could not have hiked the hike or written the words without Kate. She gave generously to this work with her time, encouragement and love. She hiked the second half of many days with me, after she moved and set up our next campground. She did all the worrying necessary for an extended wilderness adventure and is a constant source of encouragement.

Disclaimer

I'm obliged to inform you here at the beginning of our journey, of the possible side-effects of your purchasing this book and to warn you of possible dire consequences that may result from something you read in this book and foolishly try to accomplish on your own. So, let me be clear.

I take no responsibility for you being lost, stuck in the sand, eating the wrong mushroom or some other wild plant because you read this book and do something foolish. You took the action that led to your dilemma or discomfort, not me, so why hold me responsible? Put your big kid pants on and take some accountability for your own actions! Sure, legally, you can sue people for just about anything today, but honestly, there aren't any jewel-encrusted chests of gold in my closets for you to come after so please inform your attorney to look elsewhere for a payday.

I am not a doctor, so it follows that you should not construe anything I say as valid medical advice or opinion. I am also not a lawyer, CPA, DDS, MBA, PhD, plumber, electrician or engineer and you definitely do not want me working on your car. If you need the services of any of the above, you would be much better served if you called on one of them for assistance rather than me, even if I happen to be close by.

You have been forewarned.

I am, however, a trained librarian with a degree in Library Science (MLIS) and my research skills and writing ability are pretty good. If I say it's a fact, it means that it's more than just a citation from any old Web page. This book has been thoroughly researched and the facts I make up support its veracity. I am a pathological storyteller and will attempt to entertain and enlighten you. Reading this book may put you at risk for a wide variety of symptoms ranging from mild amusement and laughing out loud, to drowsiness, sleeplessness and a whole range of emotional traumas.

Further, if you do decide to go hiking on the Michigan Shore-to-Shore Trail (or any other trail for that matter), do yourself a favor and do some basic preparation. See your doctor and make sure that your heart is ready for walking in the sand, slogging through some mud and climbing up a long incline. Get a AAA membership, buy some medical insurance, exercise, eat right and have regular bowel movements before you set out on some half-baked trip into the wilderness where you don't belong. Use some common sense people! Seriously!

In addition, in an effort to be totally transparent and win your trust, so that if I ever run for public office I won't have to deal with a scandal for fiduciary malfeasance, I offer the following in a spirit of full disclosure: this book is filled with links to Amazon and other sites where I will be paid buku bucks if you buy the products I mention. I do this as a service so that you won't have to do anything except click on a link to check out a great book or something else I recommend.

I think this is only fair because you hear about them from me and it won't cost you more by following a link. So, get out there and spend some money and help get this country back to work! Unlike some independently wealthy tycoons who hoard their millions, I make it my mission to send all the little soldiers of my income back out into the economy to bring home consumer goods to Papa. So, click those links with confidence that your hard earned dollars are going to be recycled and used for good, not evil.

And thank you, in advance!

This is *my* book! You may not copy it in whole, in part, or even a little bit without written permission from the author, me. That's called copyright and I own it for this book, so there. Write your own book. Okay, you can quote from it if you use these little marks " and cite where you got it from so lots more people will buy this book and all the other ones I will write that I haven't even thought up yet.

Finally, should you or any member of your party be caught with this book in a public place, feel free to make sure that the title is clearly visible to all and to announce that it is available on Amazon as an eBook, as a paperback, or as an audio version for very reasonable prices.

Again, and finally, thank you!

Will Swartz
The Author

Author's Note

I suppose the idea to hike from one side of Michigan to the other began like a lot of things in my life do; reading books. For years, I have vicariously hiked alongside numerous hiker/authors as they trudged away toward some faraway destination trying to find whatever it is that set them out on their angst-filled journey. *A Walk Across America*, written by Peter Jenkins, resonated with me and thousands of other young college students trying to make sense of their existence. His was a journey spurred by disillusionment and fueled by discovery. Books like Bill Bryson's *A Walk in the Woods*, *AWOL on the Appalachian Trail* by David Miller, *Hiking Through* by Paul Stutzman and more recently *Wild* by Cheryl Strayed are probably responsible for influencing more people besides me to get about their own quests.

Like many, I have wanted to take on a longer hike but was never quite able to find the extended period of time that it takes to get to the doing part. Life happens. College, graduation, marriage, babies (five of them!), jobs (lots of them -- teaching, coaching, sales, marketing, management, training, school administration), moving (seven moves in two years at one point), sporting events (my own and then our children's – we have a history of 32 years in the bleachers watching at least one child or more play a sport!), not to mention all of the numerous family get-togethers, social events, tragedies, sickness etc., that our lives are filled with.

A two week trip to Isle Royale with a friend and our sons was the longest venture I had been able to put together until this hike. Even then, we managed a mere six days and only 30 some miles on the island after we spent four days traveling, camping and fishing at other locations along the way.

When people find out that I have hiked from one side of Michigan to the other, the responses are interesting. A certain number of people give me an incredulous look and make polite conversation. Inwardly I know they are saying to themselves, "That's a crazy thing to do! Why in the world wouldn't you drive?" Several times I have found myself replying, "Yes, I know I could have driven to Mackinac City and hiked from Lake Huron to Lake Michigan in about ten minutes crossing under the Mackinac Bridge." Funny.

But many responses remind me of my own when I finished one of the books mentioned above. Their faces light up and exclaim something like, "Wow, I'd like to do that some day!" or "That's awesome. How far is it? How long did it take?" And the questions continue with genuine interest. If you are one of those people, I wrote this book for you because I know that you are a dreamer and a doer like me.

Perhaps you've thought about joining the estimated 1,200 or more people who through-hike the Appalachian Trail each year. Or, it may be a different trail that appeals to you or even an entirely different mode of travel, like kayaking or bicycle touring. Maybe it will be a trip following Lewis and Clark's trail (see *Undaunted Courage* by Stephen Ambrose for a great account of their journey). Perhaps you will recreate Eustace Conway's horseback ride across America, (*Last American Man* by Elizabeth

Gilbert). There are a million adventures out there waiting for you.

Before you take on that next adventure, however, I'd like to invite you to consider the *Michigan Shore-to-Shore Riding and Hiking Trail* (from this point forward, I'll normally use the shorter "STS" so this book doesn't end up being longer than *War and Peace*). You may never have heard of the STS, even if you live in Michigan. It has been in existence for more than four decades and there is still a scarcity of information about it. If you live in Michigan, you are not more than three or four hours travel time from the trail and, if you are visiting from another state or country, it is well worth the journey.

When I decided to take this trip, I began looking for resources like maps, trail guides, magazine articles, books, etc. Now, I'm a trained librarian, skilled in the nuances of advanced Boolean search terms and able to call upon the mysteries of Dewey Decimal to the fourth decimal place. Despite the use of my super powers, there was little to find. That's because I believe there may exist a nefarious plot to keep this trail a secret.

If you are considering doing a longer term hike like the Appalachian Trail or the Pacific Crest Trail, the STS is a great one to consider hiking as a warm up or practice run, especially if you have never hiked for more than a weekend or a few days at a time. The STS is long enough to give you a good idea of the rigors of hiking, your level of preparation, and is a really beautiful trail to do it on.

The STS is easily one of the most accessible, beautiful and enjoyable trails in the Midwest, if not the USA. Yet, during my nineteen days of hiking on the trail, I did not see a single human being on the trail and only two horseback riders (and they

were just out for an afternoon ride, not crossing the state)[1]. I've reflected on this a great deal because the trail is obviously being used. It is a well worn path, but has nowhere near the volume of hikers and horses I expected. I had visions of passing other hikers during the day headed to the opposite shore, sharing trail information, camping locations, or even just a simple nod to a fellow traveler. But, instead, it was a solitary trek.

I did meet people along the way at several of the campgrounds, so the trail is not so isolated as to make you want to create imaginary objects to talk to like Tom Hank's 'Wilson' in the movie *Cast Away*. Unless you are camping out on the trail itself, you will see people in the campgrounds, on the rivers tubing and boating, and in the towns you pass through.

From a hiker's perspective, what I really could have used are the things I will share with you in this book and the companion guide, *Hiking the Michigan Shore-to-Shore Riding and Hiking Trail: A Section by Section Guide*. If you are planning to hike the STS, these books will help. If you're not, I am warning you now that there is a good chance that you will want to by the time you finish this book.

---

[1] Technically, I didn't see anyone on the STS. I did, however, meet Pat, a North Country Trail volunteer, coming east on a section of the North Country Trail that runs parallel to the STS. In this particular spot near Kalkaska, the STS and North Country Trail intertwine and cross each other several times. I was hiking along and was startled to see someone walking through the woods toward me. The section we were in was an area of heavy waist high ferns, so it appeared that the hiker was wading through them when, in reality, we were both on trails and not impeded by them at all. I called out to him and we stopped to talk. I found out that Pat was a volunteer for the North Country Trail Association (he was even wearing A North Country Trail T-shirt!) and responsible for about 100 miles of the trail. He was out hiking a four mile section that day to check on conditions, to note possible projects and to just enjoy hiking.

Finally, for more information, visit the **STS Trail Website**:
http://michiganshoretoshoretrail.com

Contents

INTRODUCTION	XXV
Overview Map	XXXI
CHAPTER ONE	1
CHAPTER TWO	13
Oscoda to McKinley Map	19
CHAPTER THREE	21
CHAPTER FOUR	27
CHAPTER FIVE	31
CHAPTER SIX	37
CHAPTER SEVEN	41
CHAPTER EIGHT	49
CHAPTER NINE	54
McKinley to Kalkaska Map	61
CHAPTER TEN	63
CHAPTER ELEVEN	71

CHAPTER TWELVE	83
CHAPTER THIRTEEN	93
Kalkaska to Empire Map	99
CHAPTER FOURTEEN	101
CHAPTER FIFTEEN	109
CHAPTER SIXTEEN	117
CHAPTER SEVENTEEN	129
CHAPTER EIGHTEEN	135
CHAPTER NINETEEN	141
CHAPTER TWENTY	147
EPILOGUE	157
A SHORT HISTORY OF THE SHORE-TO-SHORE TRAIL	163
CITATIONS	169
INDEX	174
ABOUT THE AUTHOR	179

Introduction

"I went to the woods because I wished to live deliberately, to front only the essential facts of life, and see if I could learn what it had to teach, and not, when I came to die, discover that I had not lived."

~ Henry David Thoreau

The last day of school is joyous. No more teachers ("They're like, so lame and bossy, and, like, where does he buy those scruffy clothes ---I am, like, sooo tired of listening to you drone on about whatever!"). No more tests ("Why do we have to learn this stuff, anyway, you know, cuz when am I ever gonna have to know what a Python Theory or whatever it is anyway?").

Your locker door stands open in a row of locker doors, like soldiers at attention. The inside compartment has your initials plastered on the back wall in blue Sharpie marker, but it is now emptied of all contents. Final exams and projects are completed, for better or for worse, and there is the overwhelming sense that you are free. Summer looms ahead with promise-filled days.

For teachers, it is even better. No more students ("Bratty, spoiled, mouthy, rude little creatures with nothing between their ears but dead gray matter that has been pounded to mush by loud rap music gushing from the headphones cemented to their heads - I am, like, soooo very done with you this year!") No more tests to grade ("Bureaucratic, state-mandated drivel filled with ivory tower curriculum objectives measured by stanines and median thresholds - I just want to puke on the teacher test booklet and go to Test Irregularity Prison already!")

Your classroom is cleaned out, the backseat of your car is full and there is the overwhelming sense that you are free. Summer looms ahead with promise-filled days that you feel you not only deserve, but desperately need.

For me this year, it was way better than anything any students or even teachers were experiencing. I was retiring. Or at least I thought I was. It was so hard to decide. There were pros and cons, as always. The list of reasons to stay included great people to work with, who cared about education and students. There was the important work being done to make a difference in their lives. And, a free lunch from the school cafeteria whenever I wanted one, well . . . Hmmmmm.

I had grown increasingly restless, however, in a new job assignment that I didn't really enjoy doing and was not what I had been hired or wired for. Either way, though, it was okay because no one knew and I didn't want it to be a big deal. No PowerPoint presentation with embarrassing pictures from my first years, where I looked younger than some of my students. No obligatory 'Congratulations Cake', with pats on the back and jokes about sitting in a rocker on the porch and with concerned colleagues leaning in to inquire in hushed tones:

"You're still pretty young to retire. Isn't this all sort of sudden?"

And, "Is everything okay, you're not sick or something awful are you?"

No, better to go out quietly without all the hoopla and fanfare.

"What does all of this have to do with a book that is supposed to be about hiking across Michigan?" I can hear you asking. Nothing, and everything.

In my final administrative job as a high school principal, I had told students in my address at their graduation:

> In May of the year I graduated, Alice Cooper had a hit single called, *School's Out Forever*! I'm sure all of my fellow senior classmates across the country were singing along with us:
>
> *No more pencils,*
> *No more books.*
> *No more teacher's dirty looks.*
> *School's out for summer.*
> *School's out forever!*
>
> I learned pretty quickly after graduating high school, as will you, that Alice Cooper's view of education was flawed. The secret is that graduation from high school does not mean that school is out forever. In fact, it's quite the opposite. It's the beginning of a whole new schooling process - that's why we call it a 'commence-ment' ceremony. The truth is that you are graduating from high school into the bigger school of what everyone calls the 'Real World'.

What I realized as I closed my office door for the last time was that I, too, was graduating this year. My march down the ceremonial aisle, however, is often seen as a withdrawal from the 'Real World' to an insulated, cocoon-like world called 'Retirement'.

In Retirement World the bluebirds of happiness chirp all day in a safe haven of comfort and relaxation. The rocking chairs are all lined with tweed wool blankets and slipper-shod members trundle from serenity to tranquility and back again. The best days on this planet can only be described as uneventful. This is a place of ending.

That's not what I pictured.

Retirement to me is like a commencement ceremony is to graduates. Certainly, it is the end of one thing, but, just as certainly, not the end of everything. In fact, it is more about beginning than about ending. It is more about the future than about the past. It is celebrating what you have accomplished, but only in the sense that now you do something else because of what you have learned or want to know.

For me it is not the epilogue of the story or even the last chapter, but rather the beginning of a new story; a new phase of life where every day begins with the question, "Whatta ya wanna do today?"

My first answer to that question is, "I want it all!"

"I want to live the rest of my life deliberately. I want to do the important things, to make valuable contributions that will make a difference in the world and leave a lasting legacy for generations to come. I want adventure and excitement, enthusiasm and passion. I want to pursue that bucket list like a man with his hair on fire and wring the neck of each item on it like it was a Sunday dinner chicken. Ride the bull, or at least run with them. Grab for all the gusto I can get and then some."

Calvin always captures it best for me:

CALVIN AND HOBBES © 1988 Watterson. Reprinted with permission of UNIVERSAL UCLICK. All rights reserved.

Not only was I retiring, but I had turned 60 in the spring. I had managed to not kill myself in a hundred different ways growing up, including stunts like shooting arrows straight up into the sky with our bows to see how high they might go - DO NOT DO THIS! - you can't see where a skinny arrow goes after just a couple of seconds of flight and you won't know where it is until it - thwwwwicks - into the ground, an eternity later, somewhere nearby! Now, the curtain comes down, the scenery changes and I make the transition from Act II of my life to Act III.

Six decades of Will, with retirement to boot, were cause to somehow indelibly mark the beginning of a new era of life in an epic way. Old Testament characters sometimes heaped up mounds of stones to commemorate epic events. The book of Joshua, for example, records eight separate occurrences where the Israelites piled up stones to memorialize events on their journey through the desert to the Promised Land. A similar pilgrimage seemed appropriate.

What I decided on was a return to the woods, like Thoreau, ". . . to front only the essential facts of life and see if I could learn what it had to teach, and not, when I came to die, discover that I had not lived."

Unlike Thoreau, however, my going to the woods would not be a stationary quest, but a trek worthy of the occasion; I would hike from one shore of Michigan to the other. Travel is a great teacher. Creation is a master teacher. Combining the two by embarking on a journey into the great outdoors seemed to me to hold the promise of great insight and learning.

Perhaps you stand at a similar crossroads in life. It could be that you're contemplating some kind of change or monumental event that has occurred or is looming over you like a cliff. Or maybe you are like me and just love to tag along as a book stowaway on adventurous expeditions. There are all kinds of reasons why you may have picked up this book. Whatever the motivation, this is my invitation to enlist in our little band of vicarious pilgrims and join us as we go for the gusto. I promise we'll have fun and I'll keep you safe.

Grab your pack and let's go!

Overview Map

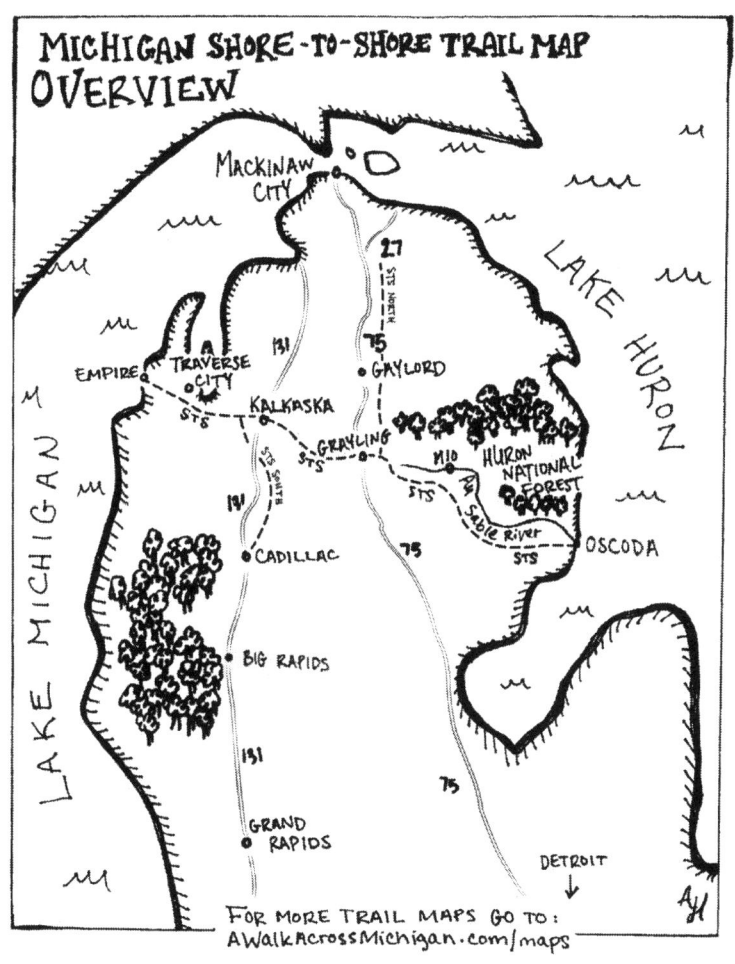

Chapter One

An early morning walk is a blessing for the whole day.
~ Henry David Thoreau

So, it looks like you have decided to vicariously hike the Shore-to-Shore Trail with me through the pages of this book. Or else you skipped the **Bonus Page, Disclaimer, Author's Note** and **Introduction.** Wow! You turned all the way here, to **Chapter 1,** without reading a word of those sections because you think this is the real beginning of the book, didn't you? If that's true, then we need to talk.

Sorry to disappoint you, but those short sections are important to read before you get to this one. "If you're going to take shortcuts in life, you'll miss some of the best stuff," (that's what Dad said). In this case, you even missed the special **Bonus Page** that's offered. It's okay though, you can go back and start at the beginning and catch up with us. We'll wait here.

While they're gone, I can see that we need to have some ground rules in place at the start of this trip to prevent anymore of this kind of thing from happening because we're going to be together for awhile and it is a loooong way to the other side of the state . . . 233.1 miles to be exact.

First of all, there will be no whining allowed. I don't want to hear any complaining about my sentence structure or my not using superlatives when describing a woodchuck or other wildlife we encounter on the trail. Or prepositions at the beginning of a sentence. You can't get cross with me because I use a fragment here or there. I'm just getting this down on paper as fast as I can sort out what the voices inside my head are yelling about and you'll have to do your part to keep up.

Second, no singing, it scares the animals away.

If you don't think you can keep up your part of the deal, then you are excused to go back to the shelf and select some other book or reading material. Perhaps a long history of the Teutonic Wars or something about crablytic cytoplasmic endosis in Rhesus Monkey societies is more your cup of tea. I'm sure you'll be wildly entertained.

To begin, you need to know something about the trail that we are going to be on. The Michigan Shore-to-Shore Riding and Hiking Trail is one of the longest continuous trails[2] in the Lower Peninsula and passes through some of the most beautiful countryside in Michigan. It begins and ends at a Great Lake, crosses through the quiet of the Huron National Forest and other woodlands, follows and crosses the crystal clear waters of rivers like the Au Sable, Manistee, and Boardman, meanders through blueberry-laden fields and gives its travelers glimpses of

---

[2] There are longer trails in Michigan, notably the North Country Trail, which is part of a 4,600 mile long trail through seven states beginning in New York and ending in North Dakota. Hmmmm. Maybe something to aim for when I turn 70!

Michigan as it was before being settled. Doesn't that just sound majestic? It really, really is!

In addition, the trail is just 'full of it' like me, as Dad says! You've probably noticed, since you're the perceptive type and this is the second time since the chapter started that I've mentioned him, that Dad is one of those little voices who has taken up residence in the back of my head and continually offers advice, opinions and comments. He'll be traveling with us because it's one way to honor him and, even though the stuff he said sometimes struck us as corny, my siblings and I have come to appreciate the wisdom he imparted to us.

Anyway, what the STS is 'full of' is history. Even the names of the places we'll be going through and near have history stuff just oozing out of the seams. For example, the STS has two major trail sections. One section, which runs north and south, begins in Cadillac. You might guess that the town is named after a car or a famous Indian chief, which are pretty solid efforts, but you'd be wrong.

This is where I employ my librarian superpowers of research to uncover the fascinating gems lying buried in those old dusty tomes lining the shelves of the back rooms of historical archives. Sure, you could look up the easy stuff and find out that Cadillac was originally named Clam Lake and that its origins, like a lot of the villages, towns and cities in Michigan, are tied to the lumbering industry. We'll learn more about logging later. But, for the really captivating stories, you have to hold your breath and dive into the dust.

The village of Clam Lake was incorporated as a city in 1877 and renamed Cadillac, after a French explorer who wasn't even born with the name Cadillac. His real name was Antoine Laumet and he is most famously known as the founder of Detroit. Antoine was an ambitious guy with a long resume that included several political appointments. He was named the commander of several forts, including Fort Michilimackinac which is a worthy tour stop at the other end of the northern spur of the STS in

Mackinaw City, 262 trail miles from Cadillac. Mr. Laumet was also appointed by King Louis XIV to a six year run as Governor of Louisiana.

One of the perks of discovering and founding cities is that you get to name stuff, even yourself. Antoine took full advantage of this benefit upon his arrival in North America. Although both sides of his family in France were prosperous, they had no claims to aristocracy. Most historians believe that Antoine Laumet de Mothe, sieur de Cadillac adopted a false lineage of French nobility when he got to the New World. Other unsavory details include suggestions that Antoine spent time in prison and there are whisperings that he was also a buccaneer for awhile.

We could further explore the doings of Sir Cadillac because he is an interesting guy and there is more to know about him, but we're wandering from the trail a bit. As a farewell to his historical legacy we'll note that in addition to the city of Cadillac being named after him, Mount Cadillac, the highest mountain in Maine's Acadia National Park, bears his name as does the luxury Cadillac automobile. And to top it all off, there's a statue of him in Detroit's Hart Plaza.

Photo by Jeremy Swartz

Back to Cadillac, Michigan. Cadillac is the Wexford County seat, but it wasn't always that way. It took the 'Battle of Manton' to achieve that designation and it's ". . . a story of bribery, corruption, intimidation, inebriated county officials and the organization of illegal townships to boost votes." An article in the September/October 2006 issue of *Michigan History Magazine* has the unabridged account of the sordid melee. We'll settle for the highlights.

The movers and shakers in Cadillac had long desired to be the Wexford county seat, which was originally held by Sherman, Michigan. Through some political maneuverings, they united with Manton, a village just 15 miles north of Cadillac, and won an 1881 election to move the seat to Manton. Just 12 months later another county-wide vote was held to determine if the seat should be moved to Cadillac. Accusations of gerrymandering and shady politics were made by the citizens of Manton, who felt they had been duped by their Cadillac neighbors. Their protests were to no avail, however, as the 'official' vote tally favored Cadillac 1,363 to 309.

The morning after the referendum, the sheriff and 20 'special deputies' boarded a train and slipped quietly into Manton on a mission to take possession of the county records and property. They had successfully loaded most of the county records and were attempting to move the first of three safes from the county building when they were confronted and driven out of town by angry Mantonites.

The Cadillackers returned home to recruit more men for a second assault on Manton. The second wave of reinforcements included city officials, several leading citizens and, most notably, several hundred mill hands. The crowd was provisioned with a barrel of whiskey and 50 repeating rifles provided by a local hardware store and they headed back to Manton.

Meanwhile, back in Manton, word had spread throughout the town and even to the surrounding farms in the area. When the Cadillac mob arrived, they were met by an equally agitated Manton crowd. As any parent knows, there are two sides to every story and both accounts in this case are, not surprisingly, at odds with each other as to what happened.

If the setting of this story had been any pioneer town in the wild west, the ending would have, no doubt, included a shoot out. Indeed, there were violent skirmishes that day in Manton which resulted in injury to the citizens on both sides of the conflict, but no one was killed. To the victor go the spoils, however, and the result of the Battle of Manton was the successful transplant of the coveted seat of Wexford county to the proud city of Cadillac.

Whoa. See what I mean by all the history? That's just the first stop on the STS that runs north and south and already we've learned some pretty interesting stuff about a town that was only 45 miles from where I grew up in Big Rapids, Michigan. The Cadillac Vikings were always one of our rivals when I was growing up and now I have a better understanding of their sketchy past. Not to disparage the fine people of Cadillac in any way. I'm sure all of this is just water under the bridge.

The main trail, for which the STS is named, runs east and west dissecting the state about two thirds of the way north of the state line. This is the one we are going to hike and, in case you forgot, it covers 233.1 trail miles. We'll start in the small town of Oscoda which, on November 6, 2006, was declared by the state of Michigan, to be the 'Official Home of Paul Bunyan'. It was given that designation because the *Oscoda Press* published the first Paul Bunyan story in 1906.

It's a contested title however, that at least five other geographical locations, ranging from Bangor, Maine to Bemidji, Minnesota and as far away as Westwood, California lay claim to. But the rationale for these other locations to be considered as Paul Bunyan's official hometown is dubious at best. Their claims are mostly linked to commercial endeavors. In most cases, extremely large statues of Paul and his blue ox, Babe, have been built and put out by the side of the road to induce motorists to stop for pictures, souvenirs or other schemes designed to deftly separate unsuspecting tourists from their money.

There's the yearly Paul Bunyan Mountain and Blues Festival in Westwood, California where a major attraction is Blue Ox Bingo. This is a blatant gambling hustle, where Babe the Blue Ox (or a reasonable facsimile), walks around until a 'chip' is dropped on a winning square. The house always wins these types of contests.

We'll hike all the way from Oscoda, on the Lake Huron side of Michigan, to the village of Empire (named after a schooner that was icebound near the city in 1865) on the Lake Michigan side. The trail cuts northwest through the Huron National Forest to the midpoint of Grayling (named after a fish we'll learn more about later), continues on a northwesterly direction passing just north of Kalkaska and just south of Traverse City, before it ends in the sands of Sleeping Bear Dunes on the east coast of Lake Michigan. One of the nice features of the STS are the ten horse camps spaced a day's ride apart across this trail.

The east side of the state is not as populated as the west side is, so there won't be as many places to stop for supplies. You can see a few small villages, like South Branch, Curtisville and McKinley on the map, but they only have a party store or a tavern to grab something to eat. Mio is the first fair-sized town (think McDonalds, grocery store, restaurants, pharmacy, etc.) between Oscoda and Grayling and it's several miles off the trail. Luzerne is a nice stopping point, with some amenities for hikers, that is accessible from the trail, but it is 90 miles into the hike.

The west side of the state, from Grayling to Empire, has lots more places that provide an opportunity to resupply, eat a good meal, or even stay overnight in a room that has real running water, toilets, clean sheets and TV. You'll appreciate things we take for granted after a few days in the woods! We'll be passing right by Kalkaska, Mayfield, Grawn and Traverse City. There's some oozy history on these cities, too, but I can tell you are getting anxious to start hiking, so history will just have to wait for us this time.

Before we start, though, there is one warning you should be aware of concerning the STS. If those who have hiked the STS were only allowed one word to describe the trail many of them would choose the word "sand". Given two words, they might say, "Damn sand!"

Since the trail has been used by horses for years it's easy to follow. Those big, beautiful animals, however, have pounded the ground into soft, sandy soil that has beach-like qualities in some places. Do you remember what it is like trying to walk fast on a hot beach to get to the water? Then you have a feel for what the sandy parts of the trail are like. They slow you down and take more effort to keep up the pace, especially on the long upward grade of a hill.

Sand is not the only characteristic of the STS, however. A lot of the trail is hardened path and soft, pine needle forest floor. In spots there are muddy patches. In a couple of places, in the low valleys, mud stretches for 30 yards or more. Horses can wade through it, but we will have to skirt around the edges. You'll be glad to have waterproof trail shoes--you are wearing them, right?

For the most part, you will find yourself hiking through a well-marked path in the woods, especially on the eastern side of the state. The quiet of the pine forests in the Huron National Forest gives it a feeling of serenity. The trees stand tall in rows that go for miles in every direction and they provide a welcome cover from the hot sun during the summer months. The trail is generally fairly flat, but has its share of long upward hills that can have a hiker with a backpack huffing pretty hard by the time they reach the top. Add the dune-like sand to a number of those uphill climbs and they become a slow, torturous test of your endurance. Are you tired yet?

Really, the trail is in the easy to moderate level of trails for hiking, which makes it a perfect first long trail to hike. It has some challenging upward hills to climb, but nothing that requires any kind of special equipment or technique. I don't think you even need hiking sticks. There are always rocks and roots that can make an ankle sprain or knee twist a possibility, but it is terrain that is very pleasant and forgiving when compared to more wilderness destinations like sections of the Appalachian Trail or the Pacific Coast Trail. No motorized vehicles are allowed, so hikers and horseback riders are the only souls we will see on the trail.

The STS is well maintained by the Michigan Trail Riders Association (MTRA-more about the Trail Riders later). Trees that have fallen over the trail, except for new falls, have been cut up and moved to the side of the trail. Even when the trail cuts through dense sections of brush, you will have no trouble following the path.

The STS is well marked in all sections across the state. The trail marker is a blue triangle with white lettering and a picture of a hiking boot print inside a horseshoe print. I think we'll make it your job to keep an eye out for them so that we don't wander off the trail.

Here is what they look like:

You'll also want to keep an eye out for posts topped with the light blue color of the trail at the trailheads and most of the major intersections, where highways and major roads are crossed.

This is what you will be looking for:

Looks like those short-cutters have caught up with us and I know you're itching to get started. It's always like that at the start of a hike; you can't get your boots on the trail quick enough.

There's one more thing to do, though, before you start. The STS doesn't have any trail registers to mark your progress, like the Appalachian, Pacific Crest and other trails do. A trail register is like the guest books some of the rest areas on the highway have. You can sign in and see where the people who were there ahead of you are from. I used to have great fun signing them with made up names, like Chuck E. Roast from Putme, Indioven or Buck Nekkid, from Needashirt, Aridzona. Juvenile. Yes, I know. Remnants of a middle school brain still firing a synapse spastically here and there.

Since this is a vicarious, electronic expedition, I set up a virtual **STS Trail Register** below, where you can mark this most auspicious beginning. You'll be able to sign the **STS Trail Register** here, at the beginning of our hike, and several places along the way. You can choose your own 'trail name,' if you'd like and leave comments for me and the other virtual hikers who come behind you. In a way, it'll be like we're all hiking together. If you leave me questions or comments I'll be able to respond to them, so you won't feel like you're on the trail alone.

I always tried to engage my students in their learning somehow when I was a teacher and that's my plan as an author, too. I think you'll enjoy this and I have some fun surprises for those who register.

Ok. As Dad used to say, "Time to fish comin' with us or what? Let's get to it!

Go to the URL below to sign the **STS**.

www.awalkacrossmichigan.com/
STSTrailRegister

Chapter Two

I held my breath as the wind caught up the trees around me in a whirling dervish. I leaned into it and struggled under the weight of an overburdened pack and pulled myself to the top of the peak. From the corner of my vision I sensed movement and narrowly evaded a falling limb, set free by the raging torrents of storm. My weary body rebelled as once again it was called upon to be the hero of the story.

Memories of the heartache that had sent me deep into the wilderness in an attempt to soothe the pain, came flooding back and wracked my already tormented mind with yet more misery. Raw emotions refused the relief of routine and, instead, waves of despair lapped at the edges of sanity and pounded the door of consciousness, demanding to be let in.

My journey to peace had begun.

Ok, not really. That's all fiction and my fertile imagination could dream up books full of awe-inspiring exploits and breathtaking feats, set in desperate backcountry situations, where, for example, chewing off an arm at the elbow is the only option for overcoming the overwhelming odds against survival. I would claw my way out of the wilderness into your hearts and you would say to your friends, "You have to read this book!"

You would soon notice, though, that both my arms are still attached.

No, in reality, the beginning of this pilgrimage was pretty inauspicious as adventures go and, actually, began before the hiking even started. A few weeks before the start date, I was vacationing at Lake Michigan with my wife Kate. We rent a house on the beach every year with my brothers, Brian and Scott, their wives, Sheila and Kim, and our sister-in-law, Andrea.

On a rainy Tuesday morning, I convinced them that a car trip to explore some coastal cities would be a great group activity. My real motivation was to get to Empire, MI., where I knew the hike would end. I wanted to explore one of the horse camps and to find out if the camps would be a good option as a place for a hiker to stay. I also hoped to see what the trail looked like.

We piled into a couple of vehicles. Three antique shops, a bathroom break and a scenic turnout later we arrived in a village that the girls described as, "Cute," "Just the most darling little place," and "Adorable, I want to live here!" That was Kate. She wants to live on Lake Michigan and misses no opportunity to try and embed that suggestion into my conscious as well as my subconscious mind.

Brian and Scott described it as, "lunch!" They always seem to be hungry when we drive. Or when we fish. Or when we golf. Or when we just ... you see how they are, yes? To be honest, which I am known for, I was a little hungry myself and the outing had been sold, in part, on the promise of food. I was a salesman in a former life and know how to subtly push the emotional buttons of my clients. With the brothers? It's just too easy!

We motored down Front Street past gift shops, antique stores and a small grocery until we spotted Joe's Friendly Tavern. It was busy, a good sign for a place that feeds people, but we were able to get a table anyway and set about selecting food and drink.

It was not an easy task, because we had inadvertently wandered into an establishment that catered to a wide range of appetites.

Warning

The following contains culinary descriptions of a graphic nature. Readers on bland diets or with overly sensitive palates may want to skip ahead to the next chapter or, at the very least, take an ice bath before preceding.

The menu was a red-light district of voyeurism, which spanned the entire range of breakfast, lunch and dinner, and offered a variety of temptations. Homemade oatmeal pancakes, grilled with dried cherries, or a smoked turkey skillet, with eggs and potatoes, made breakfast a tantalizing option, even though it was lunch time.

Zesty-spiced, crunchy, delicious zucchini treats, called out my name, in a sultry way, insisting that I, "Try them with our tangy 'Boom-boom' sauce." I resisted the siren call of the first item that spoke to me and moved on to the next temptation.

"Dark sweet cherries add a touch of sweetness," said the classic wing sauce on the eight jumbo quarters of the Empire Wings, in a shameless attempt to take me out on a date.

I kept my desires in check, knowing that one, or perhaps both of my brothers would be unable to restrain themselves from the lurid seductions of the tasty morsels. Surely, that meant that I too would soon be holding one of the tasty nibbles --oh, so careless are they in minding their plates!

I'm not a vegetarian, but I was tempted to convert temporarily when I saw Homemade Vegetarian Cake, standing all by herself. "I'm a blend of rolled oats, dried cherries, sweet corn, red onion, red beans, garlic & tomato," she teased, "And, I'm grilled and served on a brioche bun."

One half-pound of fried smelt, homemade chili, and a whole section of healthy looking salads jumped onto the runway, vying for my attention. I held out for the belle of the ball. My virtue was rewarded when I arrived at the full-page Burger Menu.

In the history of seduction between Man and Burger, I don't believe I have ever read a more tantalizing proposition than this:

There is a reason the burgers at Joe's are so good. We start every day in our own butcher shop with the highest quality two-way chuck and cut and grind it to 80% lean (let's face it; a truly great burger has to have some fat). Rest assured, the hamburger you eat today is the absolute freshest burger available. We put more effort in making sure your burger is fantastic than most places put into their whole menu. Our burgers are award-winning and have been featured in articles by the New York Times, Wall Street Journal, Flint Journal, Lansing State Journal, Traverse City Record-Eagle, Traverse The Magazine, the Detroit Free Press, the Leelanau Enterprise and recently we were named Best Burger in Northern Michigan by TV 7/4 in a "Your Town Showdown," beating all comers! Simply put, Friendly Burgers are the best!!!

Here was an enticement to throw caution to the wind and I'm not ashamed to admit that the ensuing tryst was everything and more than I could have desired. I know it was good for me; for the salacious burger and sweet potato fries that beguiled me, I'm pretty sure it was just a one-night stand.

The spot we were sitting in had originally been the company store for a lumber mill way back in 1887. The mill burned down twice, once in 1906 and then again in 1917, before the company finally threw in the towel. The company store fell into disrepair, was razed and then rebuilt as Friendly Tavern, in 1940 by Chet Salisbury. It shared a space with Chet's other commercial endeavor, a hardware store.

I'm always intrigued by the interesting combinations of businesses you find like that, especially in smaller towns. Blending a hardware store and a restaurant-tavern serves the needs of the populace by providing important services and resources that aren't available anywhere closer, but what a change of hats it must take to go from asking in the restaurant, "Would you like a pound or two of nails with your burger and beer?" to suggesting in the hardware, "How about some smelt and a salad with your 100 percent silicone, permanent weatherproof caulk?"

Eccentric pairings of perfectly rational stand-alone businesses are numerous once you begin to take notice of them and I've started a collection that you can add to when you spot something quirky (email me at:

Weird@awalkacrossmichigan.com

You may think that a laundromat/pharmacy, a restaurant/bait shop, a veterinarian clinic/party store, or a florist/tux rental/coffee shop/gift store are just examples I made up, but only one of them is. The other three are in business today.

Friendly's didn't add "Joe's" to the name until Joe Wiesen purchased the establishment in 1974 and moved to Empire with his wife, Kathleen, and eight children. Joe's smiling picture is still above the bar even though the business was sold in 2006. Today, Joe's Friendly Tavern is owned by Frank, Mary, Max, Henry and Gemma Lerchen. The history, menu and pictures of the restaurant are online at: **Joe's Friendly Tavern**[3].

If you happen to visit Sleeping Bear Dunes, just outside Empire, be sure to stop in for a meal at Joe's and don't forget to tell 'em Will sent you! (That should be good for free food the next time we visit!)

"Do you know where the Shore-to-Shore trailhead is," I asked our waitress when she brought us our checks. My question was met with a blank stare and her deflection, " Ask John, the bartender. He lives here all year long and will know that kind of stuff."

I approached the bartender with the same question. He looked puzzled and I explained further about the Shore-to-

---

[3] http://www.joesfriendlytavern.com/about-us.html

Shore Trail being a horse and hiking trail maintained by the Michigan Trail Riders Association. A light went on and he said that he had seen a bus with that on the side of it. He didn't know where the trail started, but he thought there was a camp somewhere east of town. Armed with such sketchy information, I envisioned that finding the trail might be a little more challenging than I first imagined.

We wandered onto the street and began exploring the nearby stores. Empire has a post office and I've learned that the people inside these buildings know lots of things about places in their town. As a staunch member of the male club that never asks for directions, I pretended to need stamps and headed across the street. The clerks were helpful and I left with specific directions to Garey Lake Horse Camp, the last of the camps I would pass on the hike and just 9.1 miles away.

The number of horse trailers and campers set up were a surprise when we arrived at the camp. There were horses tied up, smokey fires ringed with family and friends, bales of hay and the inviting smell of meat on the grill. As we drove by, we could hear bits of conversation and muffled laughter that is the ambience of summer in a Michigan campground.

Garey Lake was a large and roomy camp and I felt better knowing that I wouldn't have a problem getting a spot to camp, even when there were organized trail rides. In fact, I thought it might be fun to get to know some of the trail riders.

As we drove by the back of the camp, I saw a blue trail marker and the path disappearing into the woods. My brothers and I piled out of the car and followed the markers for a short distance on the trail. I didn't know then how much I would appreciate arriving at this very spot several weeks later.

Oscoda to McKinley Map

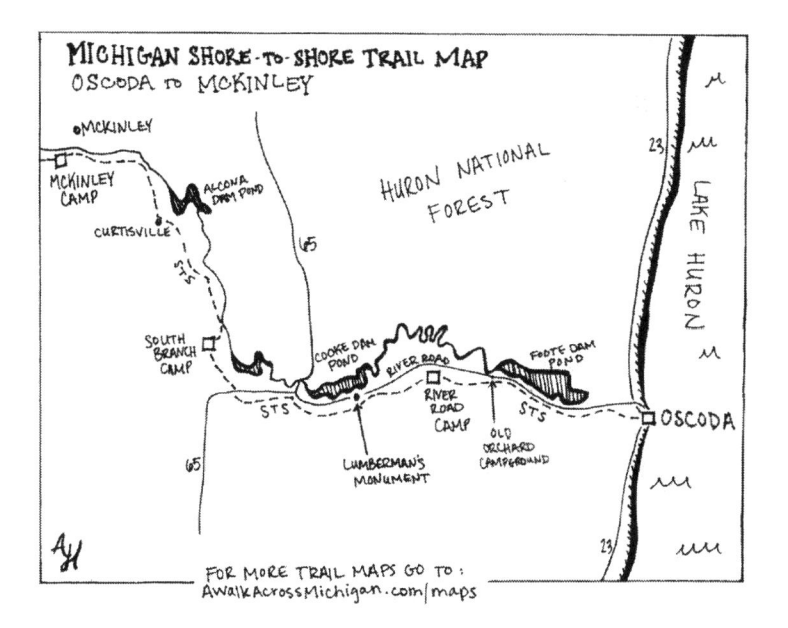

Chapter Three

Never look back unless you are planning to go that way.
~ Henry David Thoreau

Kids, "*Are we there yet? Are we there yet?*"

Parents, "*Just a little farther, sweeties. It's just a little bit farther.*"

Readers, "*But Will, we're still not hiking on the trail yet! It's been a Disclaimer, a Bonus Page, a Note from the Author, an Introduction and two chapters and we haven't logged a single trail mile yet.*"

Will, "*Just a little bit farther, sweeties. Don't be in such a rush. Enjoy the journey. That's what Dad always said.*"

The house was locked, the lights were off (I went back in and checked, twice), the windows were closed, and the snacks were in the car; I had my wallet, reading glasses, sunglasses, and hat; Kate had the extra keys, magazines to read, extra lip balm (she always has at least one), and a couple bottles of water; my pack was packed; the car was loaded and gassed. Anticipation had climbed to the top of the mountain and was ready to base jump into the void. We were completely ready to start the adventure. And the radiator was leaking. Of course.

Luckily, I have a Tony.

That's because Dad had a Chuck. When I was growing up, we always took our cars to the same garage and always entrusted the repairs to Chuck. Over the years, Chuck and his wife, Charlene, became good family friends and I remember them sitting at our kitchen table on weekend nights, playing cards, laughing and sharing life together. And, over the years, our cars always got great care and repair at Chuck's Service Station.

Tony owns and runs Canton Auto Repair and Exhaust. It's conveniently less than a mile from our house and Tony takes great care of me and my cars, like Chuck took care of my dad and his cars. If you don't have a Tony and something like a radiator leak happens just as you are leaving on an adventure, you call the dealership repair shop and they say they will be happy to have you bring in your vehicle for them to inspect and repair--a week from this coming Tuesday!

Tony is only one player on Team Will. I also have a Roger (handyman), a Randy (lawn care), a Dustin (pool guy), an Adam (financial planner), an Angie (CPA and taxes), and a Phil (editor). You might think that I live a pretty pampered life with all these people providing services, but I'll have you know that I have really cut back. In fact, I used to have live-in maids, butlers, chauffeurs and dishwashers. Unfortunately, they all moved out to start their own families and I've not been able to replace them at the same rates.

I also have a Kate. She's my Sherpa, for this trip anyway. She envisioned her role as being my personal support team, like the Sherpas, who do all the heavy lifting for the climbers at Everest. Not exactly a fun way for her to spend vacation days, even if we did get to be together. Kate had agreed to drive me to the trailhead and camp with me for the first two nights. She would set up camp while I was hiking and make dinner. In the morning she would help get me on my way and then move the camp to our next spot. That way I could just hike and not even have to carry a 45 pound backpack. It would let me ease into the hiking part of the trip.

We limped our leaky radiator down to Tony's shop and told him our predicament. An hour later, we were on our way to Oscoda. Sure, he may not have been busy that morning (not likely), but being a good customer has its advantages.

The trailhead on the Lake Huron side of the state is just as difficult to find as it is on the Lake Michigan side. I've arrived at the conclusion that there are three reasons why the STS is not swarming with hikers:

- ➢ The big boy trails, like the Appalachian and Pacific Crest, have lots of books written about them, including trail guides where you can find detailed descriptions and the exact longitude and latitude coordinates for key locations --including trailheads!
- ➢ The words, "Michigan Shore-to-Shore Riding and Hiking Trail," will only fit on a 6X-size Tshirt, so there isn't enough advertising and marketing.
- ➢ The trailhead at either end of the trail is a mystery spot and a closely guarded secret that is only revealed to those who stumble upon it.

We began by driving up and down the closest roads to the lake, looking for one of the trail markers. The map from the Michigan Trailriders Association showed the starting point, but there didn't seem to be anything resembling a trail post or blue triangle trail markers, and there certainly wasn't a trail anywhere in sight.

The parking lot of a city park, which also backed up to the Oscoda Chamber of Commerce, was the only thing there.

Putting the man card concerns aside, I went in to ask for directions. The lady at the desk didn't know anything about the STS but a manager in the back office overheard us talking and came out to help.

"When the horses come," she said, "we open the gate down to the lake and they all ride onto the beach and touch the water and then go that way."

She pointed me in the direction they would head across busy Highway 23 into the neighborhood across the street. Kate and I headed down to the water for some quick pictures to document the start of the hike. A few minutes later, I waved to Kate from the other side of the highway and watched as she drove off to find our campground for the night. At last, I was finally hiking the Michigan Shore-to-Shore Trail.

Or at least I thought I was. I hiked into the neighborhood and just followed the first street that headed west. No waving crowds. No bands playing. No big send off party. No trail markers. And, hiking on a paved street. Except for the water pack and trail clothing I was wearing, no one would have known that I wasn't just out for a leisurely stroll through the neighborhood, but was instead fixed on walking across the state.

The street came to an end and there was only one way to go,

so I turned right and headed north. Four blocks later, tucked into the middle of a neighborhood, on the corner of Old US 23 and Third Street, the first visible symbol of the STS, a blue-tipped trail post, announced that I was, indeed, on the trail. The blue trail marker attached to it pointed me west again and I hiked on, with a smile on my face.

A few blocks later, the road ended abruptly and I stepped into a green woods that was a different world. It was filled with the serenity that I was seeking. This was what the trail was supposed to look like. Trees and green things growing everywhere with a pleasant path that threaded through the pines. Birds and little creatures rustling in the leaves. All my anxious thoughts disappeared.

The blue triangles came and went every few hundred feet as the pace and trail became comfortable. For quite some time I continued on being comfortable and that's when you have to be careful. When the trail popped out onto that busy road you didn't notice, either, did you, that we were supposed to cross it instead of hiking down the shoulder. It's a common mistake.

Trucks were whizzing down the road beside me, creating hot blasts of wind that buffeted me as they went by. A driver or two waved as they went by and I waved back. Northern Michigan is so friendly. I was two miles down the road before realizing there hadn't been a marker. I pulled out the trail map and it was easy to see where I had gone wrong.

I hate to go back, but Dad says, "If you hike the wrong way, it doesn't matter how long you hike, you won't get to where you're trying to go." A corollary to this is, "Hiking faster in the wrong direction will only get you to the wrong place quicker."

I looked at the map and made the decision to do a couple more miles of road hiking (I hate road hiking), cut back north another mile on the road and then get back on track where the trail crossed the road again. The penalty for not paying attention, in this case, was sizzling out on the hot tarmac instead of enjoying the cool of the green forest. This was a good lesson to pay attention at any kind of junction.

Nevertheless, the first day proceeded without anything more than a missed turn and some extra hiking. Kate met me at our agreed upon pickup point and the first miles of the trail were behind me. The highlight of the day, however, was still to come and was waiting for me at the campground Kate had found.

Chapter Four

Live the life you've dreamed.

~ Henry David Thoreau

When we pulled into camp site 21A, Kate had a surprise waiting for me. Our six-man tent was set up with sleeping bags and gear already inside. But it wasn't at the primitive horse camp I thought we would be at for the night. Instead, Kate had found Old Orchard Campground, an upscale luxury condo with all the amenities compared to what I had anticipated.

Even better, there was a bundle of dry, split fire wood on the ground beside the fire pit. Most welcome of all, however, was a bucket of Kentucky Fried Chicken, a dinner for four, set up on the campground picnic table waiting for the diners to be seated. The significance of that fast food banquet will not be apparent without a short visit to the past.

I started the hike on July 8, our 36th wedding anniversary. It was a strange sort of way to celebrate an anniversary, I realize, but reminiscent in so many ways to our start as a couple. When we were married on 7/8, 1978, between 7 and 8pm (It is SO easy to remember our anniversary date!), life was pretty simple. I had just graduated from college with a teaching degree. We didn't have an apartment or place to stay and nothing keeping us, so we took the money we received as wedding gifts and headed out on a honeymoon road trip, with California as the eventual destination. Looking back, I'm sure our parents thought we would soon be living in one of their basements.

Free as tumbleweeds and just about as directed, we drove wherever the roads headed west, exploring whatever caught our fancy. We made it as far as Glacier National Park and fell in love with the mountains. We stayed for a week, camping and hiking in the backcountry.

It was a magical time. We touched snow in July and survived a night time attack by what we thought at the time were ravaging grizzly bear cubs.* We got a room in a lodge that had no rooms available. The manager at the desk took pity on us as newlyweds and put us in a room that served as a closet (literally!) for the maids. Cover your ears, kids, for this next sentence. We spent two joyous nights giggling and cuddling in the closet as people walked just feet from our heads.

On our first day's hike into the wild we came to a waterfall and, on my first cast into the pool below it, caught a trout for our dinner. Proud fisherman and provider for his woman! Kate is always quick to add to the story that, while I was fishing in the distance, a couple of guys hiked by and commented to her that they wished they could find a woman who would follow her man up into the high country backpacking and camping!

The best dinner on that entire trip, though, was not the fresh caught trout on a campfire. Nor was it the outstanding grilled steaks we enjoyed at a mountain lodge restaurant. No, our favorite meal was the entire KFC bucket of chicken with all of the sides designed to feed a family of four that we devoured at the beginning of our honeymoon on the shores of Lake Michigan.

I don't think I have to tell you what the best meal I had on this trip was. We enjoyed an excellent fried food feast and sat around watching the embers of the fire glow. As the sun turned red and dropped into the horizon over the lake, I gently took Kate's hand and led her to the tent.

In the dim light ... Ok. Ok. Fade to black. End of chapter.

* This was probably brought on by reading *Night of the Grizzlies* in our tent late at night. Marmots, we found out later, were the night time marauders that we mistook for grizzly cubs. They're cute little critters that look like a cross between a woodchuck and a prairie dog. In the morning, we discovered that the varmints had chewed a hole into the corner of our tent, dragged my leather belt out and chomped off a hunk of it as an appetizer. I'm sure we would have been the main course for the hungry horde if I hadn't bravely fended them off with my flashlight!

Chapter Five

"I can alter my life by altering my attitude. He who would have nothing to do with thorns must never attempt to gather flowers."

~ Henry David Thoreau

Ahhhh. Early morning in a Michigan campground in the summer. The creaky doors of tent campers and noisy tent zippers in the quiet. Hushed stirrings of the early risers as they shuffle to the showers and to morning ablutions. Wispy smoke trails rising from new fires. The clank of pans and cooking that creates a smell that's able to draw even the sleepiest camper from the cocoon of a sleeping bag: bacon!

Kate was still a cozy, sleeping mound of blankets as I crept out of the tent. Sore muscles moaned in protest when they realized they were moving. It was still cool during the nights and early mornings and the air felt brisk on bare legs. I walked down to the edge of the bank overlooking the backwaters of the river on the Foote Dam.

The Au Sable River is a truly amazing river. A 1795 United States Gazetteer originally labeled it the "Beauais River," but the literal French words, "au sable," meaning "with sand," were a more accurate descriptor and quickly became the recognized name.

The 138 mile long waterway begins north of Grayling and flows west to east through the city of Grayling, then to Mio, and then spills into Lake Huron at Oscoda. The Michigan Department of Natural Resources has designated it as a Blue Ribbon Trout Stream and it is one of the best brown trout fisheries east of the Rockies. The 23 mile stretch from Mio to the 401 bridge has been recognized as a National Scenic River. Pretty high praise.

The early lumber industry saw a different kind of beauty in the river. It flowed through the incredible forests of white pine for long, straight stretches; a perfect highway for floating logs. The river served for years as a route to send millions of board feet of the highly prized timber to market.

Two brothers from Adrian, Michigan, William and James Foote, also saw beauty in the Au Sable, in the sheer power of moving water. Their vision resulted in a series of six hydroelectric dams on the Au Sable that eventually became a part of Consumers Power and today is Consumers Energy. Foote Dam was named after William and is nine miles upstream from Oscoda. Old Orchard Campground, where Kate and I were camping, spreads out for almost four miles along the banks of the Foote Pond behind Foote Dam. It's one of several gorgeous campgrounds along the Au Sable.

Kate, also, saw the beauty of the Au Sable. The river, the green forests, the wildlife, and the splendor of it all was a powerful mixture. It created a peaceful tranquility that I saw in her eyes as we sat quietly in our camp chairs in front of a fire, watching the sun set over the water. Blending a large body of water with a red sun dropping over the horizon does something to her, especially if it is anything like the one we watched from the dunes at Lake Michigan, just before I proposed.

In addition, the unexpected luxuries of hot showers, toilets, electric hookups and running water in the campground were making our stay enjoyable rather than something to endure. The five dollars more to stay in lavish, luxurious surroundings rather than the primitive camps I had described were a surprise to both of us.

I saw Kate see the beauty and I saw instant bonus days for Sherpa service!

My original plan for hiking the STS was to backpack the entire way. Kate had agreed to two nights of car camping to get me started and then she was headed home. She had a mental image of this trip being more of the grimy outdoors than what she cares for--the one with smoke in the eyes, insects buzzing around your head and stinky body parts. Kate's always good for a night or two on the trail or camping, at whatever level, as long as she knows that we'll be somewhere she can get a hot shower and she will not be sleeping on the ground by that third night.

I heard the zipper to the tent and watched as Kate emerged, her curly hair tousled. She waved hurriedly and headed toward the bath house on a mission. I looked back out over the glass-calm water and my thoughts turned to the mental wrestling match that was going on in my mind over retirement.

For 26 of the 28 years I had spent in education as a teacher, coach, librarian, media director, preschool director and, lastly, alternative high school principal, I had enjoyed going to work. Life was good. My days were filled with a variety of projects and tasks that were a good fit for my interests and abilities. I was working in the district where my own children went to school and it was fulfilling to know that my work benefited them. I would probably have blissfully continued for several more years until I couldn't toddle into the building anymore except . . .

Life changes.

I remembered being summoned to the Assistant Superintendent's office after returning from vacation at the end of July almost two years before. "The two jobs you are currently doing, Director of Media Services and Preschool CoDirector, are being eliminated because of financial cuts and you are being assigned as the new Director of Alternative Education," said the assistant superintendent.

"Wow," I thought. "This doesn't seem, to me, to be the best use of my talents. I have no experience as a principal or vice principal or any position dealing with student discipline and here I am being placed in a job where most of my day will be spent managing students in conflict and leading a mostly veteran staff, who know way more than I do. If this was a position that was posted, I wouldn't even be called for an interview."

In the back of my mind, Dad said, "You can't control most of what happens in life. What you can control is how you respond to what happens." I could have quit and gone elsewhere to do a dozen other things, but there were more reasons to stay than leave and I responded by taking on the challenge of a new assignment.

I failed at a lot of things that first year, but, sometimes, that's how you learn. "Failure is not final." Tony Robbins said that, though I'm sure he must have talked with Dad, too. I learned new skill sets, adapted processes and programs, solved financial and facility problems, worked to resolve staff issues and, always, always, dealt with constant and sometimes overwhelming student discipline issues. Most of all, I worked my butt off.

What was rewarding, despite all the challenges, was the progress that we made with students. The stories of these young people were filled with heartbreak and tragedy. Broken homes, screwed up relationships, poverty, sex and pregnancy, drugs, poor decisions, truancy, violence, shootings, crime--the list could go on--created consequences in their lives that landed them in an alternative school. It was no surprise that academic performance was way down the list of their concerns.

The talks I had with individual students were the best. It became evident, very quickly, that many of them needed more than just an alternate approach to education. They needed a whole range of resources that dealt with everything from counseling to social services as well as academic support. Most of all they needed to be loved.

It turned out that the kind of advice my father had given me, when I was growing up, and that I had passed on to my own kids, was exactly what these kids needed to hear. In fact, as the year went on, I felt like I was channeling Dad as I shared with them the necessity of getting a high school diploma, honesty and good character, hard work, discipline, attitude, the importance of learning and many other issues. There were difficult conversations about change and accountability. My messages to the students served as personal motivation and self-therapy as I faced my own challenges.

The reward for all of this struggle and conflict was seeing young people make positive changes. They didn't all change, and it was always a struggle, but it was worth all of the turmoil to watch as the light bulb clicked on in their minds and they got it; to see them finally stop banging their heads against the wall and get their lives together.

The second year was vastly improved over the first. I had stretched and grown as an administrator, gained new skills, studied and read widely in areas where I needed more knowledge. Better processes were put into practice. I managed to redirect grant money to add paraprofessional staff. Student discipline referrals and suspensions were less than half of what they had been the previous year. One staff member told me that it had been one of the best years of her career. The building was calmer and I knew that if I stayed on it would continue to improve. Life was good.

I had turned the corner in this new role and felt confident that I could, in time, excel at it, as I had in other positions. I could do meaningful and rewarding work in this setting and the need for people who genuinely cared for these students was apparent.

But, I was retiring, right?

When Kate returned from the bath house, I was sitting in a chair looking at a trail map. The hike for the second day was intentionally planned to be a long one to maximize the time I wouldn't have to carry a backpack. The trail section between River Road Horse Camp and South Branch Horse Camp was 19 miles on the map. It would be a chance to see if all of the conditioning I had been doing at Orange Theory (an intense 1 hour, trainer led, interval workout) and at my local gym was going to pay off.

We had a quick breakfast and drove to my starting point for the day. It was nice not having to pack up everything or take down the tent. One of the benefits of car camping while hiking was being able to stay at the same camping spot for several nights and drive to the drop off and meeting points.

As I got out of the car, Kate confirmed our meeting point for the end of the day and then she took off on her own adventure. She wanted to explore the area and tour something called the "Lumberman's Monument," before hiking in from the end of the trail to meet me. She had grown up with a family that stopped at historical markers along whatever vacation route they took. There was no doubt I would soon know more about the Monument and its history.

It was sunny again and promised to get warmer as the day progressed. My own challenge for the day seemed simple compared to all of the turmoil of school. A 19 mile walk in the woods. A chance to reflect and think, renew and refresh.

The trail was peaceful and scenic. The predominant color was green, which made the contrast of the wild flowers and plants that much more striking. The woods are always a cooler place to be and, even in July and August, can be ten degrees less than anywhere else. Wildlife is abundant on the trail and there are always the rustlings of squirrels, chipmunks and other small birds and animals just off the path. I stopped and listened intently as something louder drew my attention . . .

Chapter Six

There was a tremendous thrashing of the brush and then all was total silence. A magnificent stag emerged onto the path directly in front of me. He stood pawing at the ground and snorting his displeasure with my presence. Desperately, I fumbled for my pocket knife and prepared for a feeble defense.

I looked closely and immediately saw that I was well to be wary, for this was no ordinary deer.

This . . . was a River Deer.

One of the same River Deer Clan that had tormented my dear mother and that knew me as a sworn enemy.

River Deer are hoodlum groups of deer that boldly venture from their riverside dwellings into the neighborhoods of the weak and elderly to pillage and ravage their green garden plots. Their brutal night time raids leave little for the unfortunate villagers to store up for the coming cold of winter. Without the bounty produced by their fertile patches of ground, most are reduced to meager rations of oatmeal and frozen TV dinners in order to survive.

My mother, Bette, had experienced their savage attacks only a few years earlier. I had learned of her plight in a phone call, when she reluctantly confessed that she had been a victim of their heinous assaults. It took me only minutes to pack my gear and head out to protect the honor of the homestead. On the way I mobilized my brothers Dale, Brian and Scott. They would meet me at our childhood home and together we would strategize and execute our plan to eliminate this blight with extreme prejudice.

At sunset the following day, we were in place and ready. As the street lights winked on and twilight turned to not twilight, the neighborhood settled into an uneasy quiet. It didn't last long. Slinking from the shadows of the river forest just three blocks away, a large gang of surly teenage River Deer headed our way. It was obvious that they'd been partying and were looking for trouble.

Trouble is what they got when they reached our garden gate. It was not a long battle, but it was a fierce one. The kind that causes weaker men to babble on about horrors and curl up drooling in a fetal position. The kind that marked me as a man with a price on his head. The kind that forever destined me as a target for . . . the revenge of the River Deer.

Now, here I was, alone, facing what was obviously the leader of a related River Deer gang, whose only thought and purpose for living at this moment, centered on exacting that revenge.

One on one. Mano a animano . . .

Oh, did I write that out loud?! Sorry.

For the second day in a row, I spotted deer. Or rather, it spotted me and bolted for cover, startling me as much as I had scared the deer. A rude, flapping salute of its white tail was all I saw of that one.

I kept a steady pace for the morning and at the three hour mark took a break for lunch. An hour later I was back at it and pushing to reach my goal of hiking between two horse camps in a day. I crossed roads at regular intervals that made it easy to keep track of progress and was encouraged to see the blue trail markers come and go.

Meanwhile, Kate was having an excellent day touring the local area and she ended it with a trip to Lumberman's Monument, a nine-foot bronze statue by Robert Ingersoll Aitkin, located at the Huron-Manistee National Forest Visitor's Center. It memorializes three lumbermen, and their historic lumbering tools, as a tribute to the logging era in Michigan.

Photo by Maurice "Moose" Gauthier

When Kate finished at the logger's memorial site, she hurried to our meeting place at South Branch Horse Camp and started her hike back on the trail to meet me. She was a welcome sight after a long day hiking and set the pace for the last two miles as we finished the nineteen mile plus section. After a short rest we headed back to the campground at Old Orchard for a good meal, and a much appreciated shower.

As we sat around the fire after dinner, Kate told me what she had learned about the logging industry in this part of Michigan. It reminded me of some interesting family history that I had recently become aware of. Earlier this year my brother, Brian, gave each of us a copy of the family genealogy that he has been working on for quite some time. Like most families, we have a few disreputable characters that muddy the waters of the gene pool but, all in all, the vast majority of our family has conducted themselves as good citizens.

Unexpectedly, we learned that our heritage is more Dutch than German, which made my 100% Dutch wife, Kathleen "VanDyke" Swartz, very happy. The Swartz name, or "Swart" as it was known in the old country, is the record of a proud, independent people and some of the contributions to society made by our ancestors make me proud to be part of the Swartz lineage and they inspire me to live up to the high standards set by our ancestors. No one more so than a distant relative I discovered that Brian had overlooked.

Further back in the records, if you look hard enough, you will find that the Swart family was related through marriage by a pair of second cousins who were twins, to another well known and respected Dutch family, the Swartzenchoppins. Buried in the annals of our dual family history I found the story of a fascinating young lad named William Hansfeld Swartzenchoppin, who, coincidentally, made significant contributions to both the lumbering and furniture industries in Michigan. As Kate shared the details of the historical significance that the lumbering industry had on the early development of Michigan as a state and to this area of the STS, I was struck by how the two stories were entwined with each other.

When I told her about the link to our distant relative, she wanted to know more. I was tired from the long day of hiking, but I knew it was important to her. So, this is a great place, after hiking twenty plus miles, to take a short educational detour. Think of it as if you were sitting around the campfire with friends and family. You can even make a s'more if you want!

Oh, --and you'll want to sit on the other side of the fire where the wind isn't blowing or you may get smoke in your eyes.

Chapter Seven

"Get your facts first, then you can distort them as you please."
~ Mark Twain

William Hansfeld Swartzenchoppin, or "Willy," as he was known by friends and family, emigrated from Holland to Maine in 1844 as a young teenager. Many of the American logging companies recruited labor in the European countries and advertised free travel for those who would work for them. Fleeing poverty and with an uncontrollable fear of the floods that often occur in the Netherlands, Willy signed the sailing papers and arrived in Portsmouth, Maine with a single pair of wooden shoes and a black cat named Cher. He had the strong physical characteristics of all the Swartzenchoppin family that made him the perfect candidate for the lumbering companies.

Willy began as a "swamper," which meant that he cleared the 25 foot roads cut into the heart of the forest of trees. He cut overhanging branches, moved rocks and filled in the low spots so that the logs could be moved down the road to a 40 foot wide area called a "skidway," where the logs were loaded on to sleds and pulled to the mouth of the river. In addition, when a tree was felled, the swampers would trim the branches off and prepare the tree to be cut into sixteen foot logs.

Willy also proved himself as a "skidder," though he reports in his journal that he didn't care for this job much ". . . because of the precarious nature of trees stacked to such great heights (sometimes 20 feet high)." A skidder's job was to use pulleys to pile the logs onto a huge sleigh and then lock them into position with a chain called a "binder."

Willy eventually became a "shanty boy," which is what lumberjacks called themselves at the time. He worked hard and distinguished himself among even the best of the men and he caught the attention of the higher ups in the company. One of those men was David Whitney Jr., who made millions in Massachusetts as a lumber baron and then moved to Detroit in 1857 to manage the expansion of his lumbering empire in Michigan. Willy and David became fast friends and, in later years, Willy often occupied a second floor room at the famous Whitney House on Woodward Avenue when visiting Detroit.

By the early 1840's, it was becoming obvious to the logging companies that the supply of pine was coming to an end in the

New England states. White pine, or "cork pine" was the preferred wood of the day for two reasons: it was a beautiful wood that was easily worked and, perhaps more importantly, it floated. Hardwoods, by comparison, were not valued because they dulled the axe blades too quickly and sank like rocks. They were often burned.

The next state in the "pine band" that had an appreciable number of trees to be logged was Michigan. It was a vast territory with natural waterways and with so much timber that many felt the supply would never be exhausted. Many of the desirable white pine stands had trees that had been growing for 150 to 200 years, stood 200 feet tall, and left stumps that were up to 8 feet in diameter.

Willy worked for a couple of years to satisfy the agreement he had made with the lumber company that paid his passage to the United States, and then he had an important decision to make. The California gold rush was on and it seemed everyone was heading to the west coast in search of fortune, including many of the men Willy had come to know on the lumbering crew.

Willy decided to stick to what he knew and his decision paid off. The "lumbering era," as it is known now, was just getting started and the industry was so lucrative that more millionaires were made in the business of Michigan wood cutting than in the California gold rushing. Mr. Whitney hired Willy as a "timber cruiser" and sent him to Michigan to scout the forests for prime timber land. His job was to do the advance work of grading trees, noting where rivers were located and getting a feel for the land so that camps and roads could be set up in an efficient way. Willy also reserved the land for the company by purchasing it in 40 acre plots, called "forties" for $1.25 an acre at the land office in Ionia, Michigan. Willy was an astute businessman even at a young age and, since his pay was in the form of a percentage of the land he purchased for the company, he was able to accumulate some prime pieces of timber rich properties for himself.

With land secured and his fortune in the making, Willy found himself in need of a job to bide time until he could finance his own logging operation or sell his interests for a profit. He went back to what he knew best and, since Mr. Whitney's logging business hadn't yet moved to Michigan, he joined Loud, Gay & Co. in 1863. Their operation had 60,000 prime acres of pine along the Au Sable River and a mill at the mouth of the river in Oscoda.

It was during this period that Willy got his lumberjack name, "Three Finger Willy", as the result of an accident. Lumbering was dangerous business and injuries that included loss of limbs and even death were not uncommon. Willy's journal entry for March 7, 1863 tells the story:

"I put mine finger where I shant have and it come off clean like a French tyrant's head under the guillotine. But I feel fortunate to be standin here alive as Pancake Petey lost his life on the same day an hour later when his head was crushed by a binder (a chain holding down the massive logs stacked on a sled) that snapped. I am ashamed that I didn't feel much sory for him as he was a hog at table, especially when cookee (an assistant cook) served pancakes and also he had a prodigious amount of lice that made him uncomfortable to be in company with."

Willy's favorite job in the logging business came when the majority of men headed for home at the end of the logging season in spring. He traded in his axe for a long pole with a steel tip and a hinged hook, called a "peavy," and began work as a "river hog" in the annual log drive. River hogs rode the logs down the waterways, keeping them moving toward the mills that would process them. It was dangerous work but also paid more, up to $3.50 per day, which was attractive to Willy.

The spring drive was a big deal and people came from all over to watch the "rollway." Logs were stacked on the banks of the river during the logging season to heights as high as 160 feet and, when they "broke rollway," the logs would go crashing down the hill in a spectacular way. There were hundreds of thousands of logs to float and it was said that ". . . you could walk 130 miles from log to log from Midland to Saginaw and never touch water or land."

By this time, Willy had a deep understanding of the lumber industry from the variety of jobs he had held. He had worked himself up to being a valued foreman and was known to be an innovator that looked for ways to make things easier and more efficient. For example, he suggested using "ice roads" during the winter months to make moving the huge loads of logs easier. Wagons with sprinklers were run over the roads at night and the next day a sheet of ice made the rough and rutted roads smooth enough to easily pull the massive loads of logs on sleds.

Another innovation credited to Willy was the use of the crosscut saw to fell trees. Until 1870, the two bladed axe was the chosen tool used to cut down the massive trees. The crosscut saw was then used to saw the downed trees into logs to be stacked. Willy experimented with using the crosscut to fell the trees and soon had two man crosscut teams competing to see who could reach the daily goal of felling 20 trees per day the fastest.

History loses sight of Willy for a brief period here, and his own journal entries for the next few years were either lost or destroyed. We do know that the lumber industry in Michigan thrived for the second half of the nineteenth century. By 1869 Michigan was leading the entire nation in lumber production and would hold that title for the next thirty years. During the 1870's there were more than 800 logging camps scattered throughout the northern part of the lower peninsula that fed wood to over 400 sawmills. The work employed thousands of men.

Willy's journals make it clear that sometime after 1868 he had moved on from the manual labor of lumber jacking and had become independently wealthy. He had probably sold the land that he owned and, like his friend and mentor Mr. Whitney, was able to sell it for up to 100 times more than he had purchased it for. It's also clear, from his earlier innovations, that Willy had an inventive mind and was pursuing interests in several areas. He had purchased a fair sized house in Grand Rapids, Michigan and, like many of the other wealthy lumber barons of the day, was having another much larger one built. His estate was on the shores of Lake Michigan.

Photo credit Randy Schaetzl[4]

The next historical mention of Willy is in regards to a controversy over the invention of "Katydids" or "logging wheels," a pair of wheels nine to ten feet tall. They were an incredible innovation that was pulled either by a team of horses or a team of oxen and allowed huge logs to be dragged along

---

[4] http://geo.msu.edu/extra/geogmich/big_wheels.html

under the axle of the wheels. They were tall enough that stumps didn't impede their progress, but, more importantly, allowed the crew to rapidly move the logs without a blanket of snow on the ground.

History reports Silas C. Overpack of Manistee as the inventor, but Willy's journals in 1873 have detailed drawings of the wheels and the two men knew each other. Silas ran a blacksmith and carriage shop in Manistee and became the first to manufacture the wheels. There is some speculation that Willy sold the idea to Silas, but it may be that Silas just took Willy's original order for a pair of the huge wheels and refined it. In any event, Willy was among at least 65 Michigan lumbering companies to use them.

A third innovation that Willy had a part in was the development of the narrow gauge railway. Although his idea of moving huge loads of logs on ice roads was effective, it had a flaw. You could only lumber during the cold winter season. One of Willy's many friends in the lumber business was John L. Wood, who was also influential and well known in developing the lumbering business in the northern woods of Michigan. John had taken a young man, Winfield Scott Gerrish, under his wing and asked Willy to help the young man with a problem. Win had a large tract of land that held massive stands of timber, but the property was considered worthless because there were no waterways whatsoever by which to transport the logs.

Willy agreed and then arranged to meet with John and Win in Philadelphia when he heard that they were also going to attend the 1876 Philadelphia Centennial Exposition. It was the first official World's Fair in the United States and it's estimated that almost 20% of the US population attended. It was at the Exposition that Willy focused on a Porter Locomotive Company 0-4-0 rod engine and came up with the idea to build a smaller gauge railway into the heart of the timber land, to transport logs out of the forest. By the winter of 1876-77 such a railway was built in Clare County, Michigan and was a huge success.

Willy was at the Centennial Exposition for an additional reason, however. One of the other business interests that Willy had been pursuing in Grand Rapids was a passion for woodworking. The abundance of lumber in Grand Rapids fueled the development of a thriving furniture industry. Willy discovered that he had an innate sense of design, which was complimented by his talent as a woodworker, and that he loved to create fine pieces of furniture. His "hobby work" naturally progressed into a business venture and he opened a furniture factory store. The Philadelphia Exposition was a chance for Willy and several other furniture makers from Grand Rapids to showcase their woodworking creations. Two of his wood carvers, F. Massett and F. Averbeck, won a prize at the Exposition for their entry of an elaborate clock woodcarving. As a result of the Exposition, Grand Rapids became renowned internationally and was nicknamed, "The Furniture City."

Willy was known as a generous philanthropist in his later years and made contributions to many causes, especially libraries, which were particularly important to him. Willy died in his eighties, in 1922, after living what was, without doubt, a creative, productive and mythical life that rivaled the adventures of many of my other fictional friends.

As I finished telling Kate the story about Willy, she asked me, knowing my propensity to stretch the truth a bit now and then, if all of this really happened. You may be asking yourself the same thing and I want to assure you, as I did Kate, that it's all there in the creative research work that I do for each of my books. If you have doubts you can ask my brother, Brian. Or, better yet, you can check it out for yourself in the very sources I used. It's all there on the Internet: **Will's Sources**[5].

After all, if it's in a book, in a newspaper, on TV, or online, then it must be true, right?

---

[5] http://www.Awalkacrossmichigan.com/sources

Chapter Eight

How did the hiker get from one side of Michigan to the other side?

Hike, drink, hike, eat, drink, hike, eat, drink, eliminate, hike, eat, drink, sleep. Repeat. Repeat. Repeat.

~ Will Swartz

Two days.
33.6 miles.
199.5 more miles to Lake Michigan.

That doesn't seem like much to cover when you look at it on paper. Looking at it from the trail, when you have to walk it, however, is different. A single mile is so much farther on foot than when you watch it slide by on a highway mile marker sign in the comfort of your car. And walking it on a trail with sand and hills and branches and bugs and brush that scratches me and rocks trying to turn my ankles and now mud and sore muscles and hot sun making me sweat into my eyes and blisters on my feet and, "Who the hell put more sand in the path?!@" . . . Oh my.

I share this because it's always the third day of anything that is the toughest. Remember the first two days of football camp with three-a-day workouts? No? How about the first two days of basketball, volleyball, wrestling or even bowling? For sure you remember that new intense physical workout you started on January 1st! It's tough. By the third day it's all mental and the novelty has worn off. Your muscles are fatigued. Energy levels wane. What was fun at first is now work and thoughts of quitting begin to creep in.

Not that I had any thoughts of quitting at this point. In fact, I was committed to doing this and I really felt pretty good. Kate and I were having a good time, I was well fed, rested and enjoying being in nature. Life was good. Except for my feet. They hurt and had started to develop deep blisters in spots even though I had good trail shoes and socks and had walked and hiked in preparation for the trip. But, there was still such a long way to go.

The South Branch Horse Camp is 27.3 miles from the next horse camp, McKinley. After two days on the trail, I knew that the distance would be too much for me to cover in a single day even without carrying a backpack. This was not a race. If it was a race, our family genetics favor full contact sprinting rather than long distance gruels. Besides, the beauty of the trail was too captivating to want to hurry past any of it.

So, as I began hiking the third day, Kate headed for a place on the map called Curtisville to see what options for camping or shelter might be available midway between the horse camps. What she found was another very pleasant surprise: Alcona Park Campground.

Consumers Power built the Alcona hydro-electric dam, originally called the Bamfield Dam, on the Au Sable River way back in 1914. Or they started to build it. World War I brought a three year halt to the project that was resumed in 1921 and Alcona Hyrdro began producing electricity in 1924. The huge backwater that it produced is one of the nicest bodies of water in the state. In addition, a variety of camping and park facilities have been created on the dams' ponds on the Au Sable that are managed by Consumers Power.

Kate again opted for a modern camping site with water and electric that had a great view of the pond. Our new home for the next couple of days was quickly set up and she made her way to our rendezvous spot and began hiking back on the trail to meet me. It took her longer than she expected to run into me because I was foraging like a winter-starved bear.

I'm an opportunistic feeder. Where I find food, I eat food. If there is a bag of cookies in the pantry and I find it, I will eat it. All of it. Your white box in the frig? Same result. I attribute my ongoing battle to maintain a weight and figure significantly more attractive than Jabba the Hut to a palate that is an equal opportunity advocate.

I am, generally, willing to try anything once if it has even the slightest appeal to my senses or praise from others. As a result, I have tried things like fish eyes (not bad, has a little crunchy part that you can either swallow or remove discretely after sucking on the eyeball goo around it), sheep's head soup (good, if you can just get past the darn thing staring back up at you from the pot), hog jowls, pickled pigs feet, chitlins and cheek meat (I'm a raving fan boy of any pork product!), menudo (good, as long as you don't know what it is) and even roast raccoon (Don't. Worst thing EVER! It was a long time ago and never again --unless you know of a good recipe).

One of the pleasant surprises on this hike was finding out that blueberries were in season and were abundant on the STS. Abundant is an understatement. The number of wild blueberry plants in Michigan is incredible. Literally, I found them covering the state from shore to shore. There were two things I saw everyday on the trail: deer and blueberries. The berries are everywhere along the trail and I saw meadows as big as football fields filled with ripe blueberries.

In case you think I am exaggerating (which I have been known to do on occasion) here's a picture:

They are smaller and sweeter, like wild strawberries are, than their cultivated cousins found in the produce section of the store. It takes a little longer to get a good handful of them, but it is well worth the effort to pick them. They are just so hard to resist. I would be hiking along in the trench-like sand of the trail and there, by my knees, would be a juicy cluster of purple-blue berries crying out to me, "Eat me! Eat me!" I usually conceded to the request! On my longest day of hiking I think blueberry picking slowed my progress by at least a couple of hours.

Another forest bounty that I encountered in abundance was mushrooms. "You can eat any mushroom once!" ranks as the famous last words spoken by a multitude of adventurous souls who are now deceased. There are a lot of varieties of mushrooms along the trail and I am sure that some of what I saw were edible, but the only good mushroom I am capable of identifying without the fear of ingesting hallucinogenics are morel mushrooms. I've been assured by credible shroomers that a springtime (Mayish) hike would likely provide the opportunity to add those tasty fungi to your freezer or gourmet pantry.

I'm sure there are other edibles lounging in the woods waiting for someone to come and forage for them, but that will have to be someone else's book. Actually, upon some checking, there are several available!

Go to:

http://awalkacrossmichigan.com/books

to see my reviews.

Kate tore me away, blueberry stained hands and mouth, from the berry buffet and we finished hiking out to the car. We were excited because her brother Kevin, and his three sons, Josh, Caleb, and Levi were coming to spend a couple of nights camping and hiking with us.

Chapter Nine

"What you get by achieving your goals is not as important as what you become by achieving your goals."

~ Henry David Thoreau

Josh is a hiking machine. A marathon runner and a fitness enthusiast, he is the kind of hiker that chews up trail miles and asks, "Is that all you got?" He once rode his bike from his house to ours to attend a family holiday dinner get together. "It was a nice morning so I just hopped on my bike and pedaled over." Sounds like a delightful little spin. Did I mention that it's just a little over 100 miles between our houses and that it takes us an hour and a half driving on the freeway at 75 miles an hour. He did it following the back roads in a tad over four hours.

Josh comes from a family that does interesting things like that, though. Their family reunions, for example, are anything but ordinary. "Pash Family Survivor" has been held annually since 2005 in Michigan, Maryland and North Carolina and was adapted from the popular TV show, *Survivor*. Each family plans the events for a particular year and the final overall winner goes home with braggin' rights. There are different colored T-shirts for each team and the theme, like "Marine Boot Camp," chosen by a family member who is a marine, varies from year to year.

The premise of the competition is that tribes are created from the participants to compete against each other in a variety of events. Some require physical speed, strength or toughness. Others are mentally challenging and some are designed to test communication skills and the ability to work together. And some are just plain nuts. After each event, the tribes have to eliminate one of their own members by voting them out of the tribe. Votes can be based on the member's performance (or non-performance) in an event, their popularity with other tribesters, or just random factors. It's always fun to watch the strategies, alliances and betrayals develop among members of the tribes.

The Pash Survivor events can be quite challenging and have included things like:

- Eat wasabi while keeping a stoic face.
- Hang from a pole like a sloth. Last one to drop wins.
- Throwing knives at a target.
- Eating a whole can of sardines.
- Scavenge for an odd collection of items (realtor's sign, tokens from a pizza parlor, an old tire, a maple leaf, a picture of your group at a remote location in the woods, etc).
- Move your gear and canoe, located on the top of a hill, to the river by running it down one piece at a time.
- Solve difficult mental puzzles, like tangrams.
- Swim across a river with raging rapids to an island without breaking a raw egg held in your hand.

Playing with family members can sometimes be brutal, as on one occasion, when each team required a driver for a scavenger hunt. One of the tribes had only a single licensed driver, who was immediately voted off by all the younger, non-driving members, even though he had just finished chaffeurring all of them around. You have to watch out for those 12-year olds!

Another vacation activity that Kevin and his wife, Rickie, like is called "Treasure Hunt." As they travel, they place 20 gold coins in a clear plastic, coin holder and hide it in a public place that they visit during their trip. Gold has been placed in four locations so far, including Glacier National Park, The White Mountains, and The Appalachians. They give five children clues to the exact location of the treasure in a poem. Here's the poem for the treasure at Glacier:

We visited Glacier National Park
A beautiful sight to behold.
While we were there, we left a surprise
Twenty-five dollars in gold.
Follow the clues and the treasure is yours,
A gift from us to you.
Just remember, all treasure is not made of gold
We also give our love to you, too.
Enter the west gate on Highway Two,
Then stop at the first turn-out on your right.
Hope you arrive during the day
And not in the darkness of night.
"Going to the Sun Road Rehabilitation Information" is what the sign will say.
Look behind it to see 5 birch trunks, now you are on your way.
Lying to the left of them a fallen tree lies on the ground.
Look underneath it carefully and there your treasure will be found.
A white PVC pipe is easy to see if you know where to look.
Hope someone didn't find it before you
Or else your treasure is already took!
GPS says that it will be found here:
N 48 30 . 789 'W113 59. 224 ' We tried to make it fun as you enjoy your day in the sun!

P.S. One of the kids found this treasure already-- in case you were checking flight tickets for Butte, Montana.

So, when Kevin and the boys arrived, we had interesting companions, who were also family members, joining our little tribe. Kevin is an engineer for a large company that manufactures cables. He's a whiz at fixing stuff. He once canoed the entire Muskegon River in a canoe that he built himself and his family lives in a house in the woods that he and his wife constructed themselves from the ground up. All three of the boys are Eagle Scouts and every family member is an experienced hiker, with trail miles logged on the Appalachian Trail, Isle Royale, the Wind Range in the Rockies, and others. It was dark when they arrived so we helped them get settled into their campsite and then spent some time catching up around the campfire before heading to bed.

The next morning we made a quick breakfast and readied our gear for the day's hike. The plan was to drive to the drop point three miles away, where I had ended the previous day. Josh decided he wanted a little bit longer hike and said that he would start from camp and meet us on the trail. He got started and then a few minutes later we piled into the car and passed him trekking down the road.

Before we begin hiking today, I need to tell you about something that I have been avoiding for several chapters for fear that you might abandon the trail. Now that you have come this far, I think you'll be able to handle the revelation even though, for some, it will be horrifying.

Let me ease you into the bad news with a song:

Ticks

"Cause I'd like to see you out in the moonlight.
I'd like to kiss you way back in the sticks.
I'd like to walk you through a field of wildflowers
And I'd like to check you for ticks."
~ From the song Ticks, by Brad Paisley

There are ticks in this paradise. If there was one pest I could eliminate from this summer hike, it would be ticks —even above deer flies, mosquitoes, bees, and other insects. The reason is that they are scary looking little critters. When you start showing pictures and talking about how they burrow into armpits and other body crevices, it's uncomfortable. When you add in the fact that ticks are associated with transmitting things like Lyme disease, it's easy to see why people get a little paranoid about going out into the wild for a nice hike.

Ticks attach themselves by burrowing face first into the skin. For the tick it must be like diving head first into a favorite dish at the buffet. Only the head is able to penetrate the skin so the butt side is sticking out. The process is not painful. It's not like a bee sting or even a mosquito bite so you probably won't even be aware of it until you actively look for them. Stop itching—there's no tick in that little fold of skin behind your knee! "Because ticks can stay attached to hosts for several days, they secrete novel painkillers, called kininases, in their saliva which help them go unnoticed." Most ticks also secrete a cement like substance that helps keep their mouth secured to the host so they are not easily flicked or pulled off.

To be honest, ticks were a problem. On the eastern side of the state the ticks were much worse, as far as numbers. I don't believe there was a single day before reaching Grayling that I did not have to remove ticks from myself and from those I hiked with. The "east side ticks", as we called them, were plentiful but, when Kate did a little research, she reported that the ones we needed to be more concerned about were the ones on the west side of the state, as they were the ones that had been identified carrying Lyme disease. Once we got past Grayling, we did not see another tick.

If you're like me, you may never have had much contact with ticks or rather they've not found you yet. I only became aware of them in the last couple of years, and this was the first time on a hiking experience that I've had to deal with them. There are five ticks that are most commonly found in Michigan. The Michigan Department of Community Health (MDCH) has an excellent guide to identify them: **5 Common Ticks**[6].

Don't let the pictures of ticks intimidate you. They are ugly little bugs, but they are easily taken care of. All you need is a tick removal tool. There are several kinds available and you can view them and my recommendations at: **Tick Tools**[7].

We started the day on a pretty section of the trail that meandered through the woods, with scenic views of the Au Sable River from the tops of the long inclines up the occasional hills. We kept a pretty fast pace, determined to give Josh a run for his money, and were surprised that he hadn't caught up to us by the time we decided to break for lunch. The afternoon passed with the same results, no Josh.

Kate was waiting to pick us up at the end of the trail section and we sat resting and waiting for Josh. When he didn't arrive after a half an hour passed, we drove back to camp to see if he had turned around and gone back for some reason. He wasn't at the campground and we decided to give him an hour to return before heading back out to look for him.

Meanwhile, Josh had not taken any wrong turns and none of the awful things we imagined had occurred. He had hiked the same trail and made up some of the distance between us, but never caught up. When he reached what he thought was our ending point for the day (it wasn't), he thought that he must have missed us somehow and wasn't sure what to do, so he turned around and started hiking back. Later, we determined that Josh had turned around just half a mile before reaching us at the end of the trail, where Kate was waiting to pick us up.

We spotted Josh hiking on the road back to camp, with a determined stride, trekking poles swinging in a steady rhythm.

---

[6] http://www.michigan.gov/documents/emergingdiseases/5commonticks_282020_7.pdf

[7] Michiganshoretoshoretrail.com/ticktools

He was carrying a fully loaded backpack and the ironman always hikes in sandals. Despite the fact that he had almost doubled the miles we hiked that day, he declined our offer for a ride and insisted on finishing what he had started. Not really that surprising. That's just Josh!

McKinley to Kalkaska Map

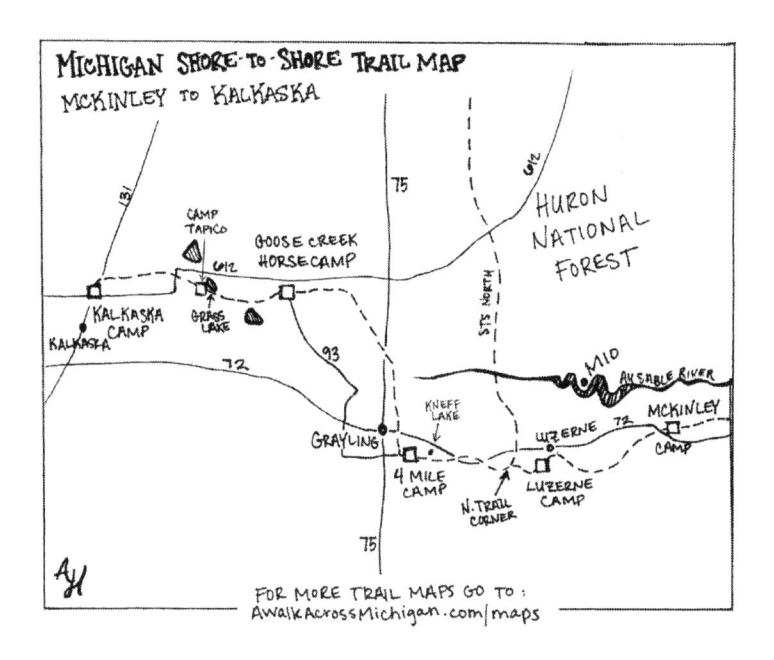

Chapter Ten

The Road Not Taken
By Robert Frost

Two roads diverged in a yellow wood,
And sorry I could not travel both
And be one traveler, long I stood
And looked down one as far as I could
To where it bent in the undergrowth;
Then took the other, as just as fair,
And having perhaps the better claim,
Because it was grassy and wanted wear;
Though as for that the passing there
Had worn them really about the same,
And both that morning equally lay
In leaves no step had trodden black.
Oh, I kept the first for another day!
Yet knowing how way leads on to way,
I doubted if I should ever come back.
I shall be telling this with a sigh
Somewhere ages and ages hence:
Two roads diverged in a wood, and I--
I took the one less traveled by,
And that has made all the difference.

During the next three days, after Kevin and his boys left, I became more and more accustomed to the daily routine of hiking. The trail veered away from the Au Sable River and the days were spent following the blue triangle markers down a sandy path through woods and fields with natural beauty that is hard to tire of.

Kate moved our camp 30 miles west to Oscoda County Park, in the small village of Mio. The village was 10 miles from the trail, but it had stores and a choice of restaurants that included a couple of those locally owned diners with good, home-cooked food that so many small towns have. In addition, it was populous enough to be worthy of a McDonalds. The campground was just a couple of blocks from downtown Mio on the backwaters of yet another dam on the Au Sable River. We felt like city dwellers, being around such a large population, and a little spoiled when we had a couple of restaurant meals instead of camp food.

My only complaint was the deep blisters that had developed on the bottom of my feet. They reminded me of the ones I had been plagued with while playing high school basketball. High top canvas Converse sneakers were top of the line technology for us and were all that we wore back then. They were hot, did little to support the ankle and double layer blisters were the norm. Our pre-practice routines included a visit to the trainer to fuse our ankles with tape, putting our feet in a powder box, and then stuffing our feet into two pairs of socks and then into our Canvas All Stars. It amazes me now that we were even able to walk. My attempts to prevent blisters were just as ineffective as our trainer's were during the season. I put mole skin on the worst spots and just endured them.

The next point of civilization after Mio was an even smaller four corners called Luzerne, where our oldest daughter, Noelle, was anxious to join us for a morning on the trail. She and her family were vacationing at a cabin near Grayling with some friends. Jerry, her canine police officer husband (a worthy candidate for any father to consider giving away a daughter to -- plus he has a boat!), had agreed to child care duties for their two girls, Emersyn and Avery, while Noelle hiked with us.

Unfortunately for Noelle, she chose the only day of the entire hike that it rained. It started raining early in the morning and it rained for the entire time we were on the trail. She slogged through the woods with Kate and I in a poncho and in tennis shoes that were soaked before she got from the car to the first trail marker to take a picture.

Rain in the woods is different than rain anywhere else. When it rains in the open meadow or your yard, you stop getting rained on when it stops raining. In the woods, when it stops raining the water on the trees continues to trickle down in droplets for a considerably longer time. It's a gentle shower and a constant dripping that makes everything clean.

The rain on this day, however, created one of the most unique experiences for us that I have ever encountered in the woods. The mushrooms came to life. Hundreds of them had pushed through the leaves and foliage on the forest floor and had a neon-like look as they glowed in the dim light of the woods. It was as though the trail that morning had led us to the surreal landscape of some medieval fantasy land, where we should be looking into the shadows for creatures like orcs, ogres and even a flinty-crusted dragon to crawl out and descend upon us.

Another creepy crawly that you may not have given a lot of thought to caught my attention that day. Off to the side of the trail was a huge mound that was knee high. Upon investigation it turned out to be an ant nest. The colony was alive with action as every one of the thousands of tiny members seemed to be on a mission to haul their huge grain of sand to the top of the heap. They would make a great advertisement for an energy drink.

Once I saw that first ants' nest I began to notice them more and more. Some were the same size as the first one, but many were much larger and must have taken a long time to build. In some places I could see several mounds within an area of a few yards of each other, like suburbs that had grown out from the main city when it got too crowded.

One of the fun things about being a librarian is that you get to learn such fascinating things. I thought it would be interesting to know more about ants so, when I got back from the hike, I did a little research. Turns out that the definitive book on ants has been written by researchers Bert Holldobler and Edward O. Wilson. It's titled, **The Ants**, and it currently lists on Amazon for $126.73. That's a pricey read, but, hey, it's a lifetime of research distilled into a book and it was a Pulitzer Prize winner in 1991. If that's too rich for your budget, the Kindle version at $120.39 may be a bargain you can't resist!

Being a very frugal collector of literature, I checked in with my local public library. They didn't have it, but a quick interlibrary loan request later and soon I had the expensive work in hand. Be warned, this is a book that will open up the world of ants like no others. It is waaaay more than you need to know about ants, but fascinating nonetheless.

Just a few facts to give you some idea of the seriousness of the issue of ants:

- There are over 10 quadrillion ants on Earth. (That's a 1 followed by 15 zeros!)
- Ants comprise from 15 to 25 percent of the earth's animal biomass.
- Ants can live up to 30 years.
- There are 12,762 known species of ants.
- The total weight of all the ants on Earth is estimated to be equal to the weight of all the humans on Earth..
- Ants inhabit every continent on earth except Antarctica, Greenland and a few islands in Hawaii and Polynesia.

I don't want to sound alarmist here, but it seems that about half of those ants mentioned above have moved to northern Michigan and now inhabit the forests surrounding the STS. I've lived most of my life in Michigan and I never realized how prolific the ant population is. Maybe it's because there are no natural predators, no anteaters, or four-year-olds with magnifying glasses, but the ants have taken over the place. They were never a problem in any way, but I thought you should know that they are there-- quietly and relentlessly multiplying in greater and greater numbers. Just so you know!

The three of us continued through the wetness and, too soon, were taking final pictures and saying a quick, soggy goodbye to Noelle at lunch time. Kate returned to camp for the afternoon and I hiked a few more miles to reach the goal for the day.

After seven days of being on the trail, we were coming to a turning point in the trip. We were almost halfway across the state and I had scheduled a day or two to rest and resupply in Grayling. Really, the intention of those days was more about having some fun in a hotel pool, finding a good meal and sleeping in a bed again. However, the halfway point of the trip was a turning point for Kate and I in another way.

Hiking is a good time for thinking. Most of the mechanics of the walking part, even on a trail, is second nature after about age four or so, which leaves a lot of brain cells to turn toward other things. One of the topics that continued to filter through my mind was the future. I had committed to myself to stick with my new role as an Alternative High School principal for two years. That would give me a chance to take on the challenge, learn the new skill sets needed for the job and to evaluate if this new field would be something I enjoyed and wanted to continue in. It would also bring me to the first point in my career where I could retire.

My position as Preschool Director had been the result of a similar change of responsibilities. I had originally been hired to be in charge of libraries for the school district. It was a perfect match for my resume, interests and abilities. We automated 17 elementary libraries in a summer, discarded old books and updated book collections, hired new staff and started new media programs. Most of all I worked my butt off. Life was good, but...

Life changes.

I remember being summoned to the Human Resources Department after that first year and given the good news: I still had a job. In fact, I now had two jobs. I would continue as Library Director, but split my time with a new position as Co-Director for the preschool. My initial response was similar to the one I had when assigned to my current position:

"Wow. That doesn't seem to be something I'm qualified to do," I thought. "My educational qualifications and background involve secondary level teaching and running libraries. I have no experience at the preschool level either as a teacher or administrator and here I am being placed in a job where most of the day will be spent dealing with preschoolers and leading a mostly veteran staff, who knows way more than I do. If this was a position that was posted, I wouldn't even be called for an interview."

In the back of my mind, Dad said, "You can't control most of what happens in life. What you can control is how you respond to what happens." I could have quit and gone elsewhere to do a dozen different things, but there were more reasons to stay than leave and I responded by taking on the new assignment.

During the first year I felt a little lost, but I discovered that preschoolers are fun. They're so interested in everything and their enthusiasm for learning is infectious. I dove into learning with them. I stretched and grew as an administrator, gained new skills, studied and read widely in areas that I needed more knowledge. When things got overwhelming, I could go to a classroom, sit at a table built for four year-olds and make clay animals. By the end of the second year, I knew that I had turned the corner in this new position. Life was good.

Now, I was at the end of the two years as Director of Alternative Education and a decision needed to be made. I thought about all of the good things that had happened because I had been willing to take on something new. I considered the rewards of working with students, the work that was yet to be done and the people I had developed strong relationships with. I also thought about a talk that I had with Toby.

Toby sat in my office across the desk from me, again. We talked, again. It was a talk I could give in my sleep after doing it so many times with so many students. The main message was advice that Dad had impressed on me as I grew up and I now passed on to those in front of me.

> *"You need to find out what you want to do in life and then pursue it. Find something you really enjoy doing and make that the work you do. Most of us are going to work for 40 years or more and having a job you love rather than one you hate will give your life meaning and purpose."*

I had advised Toby of the importance of having a high school diploma, that it is the door to everything else he wanted in life. "It leads to further training at whatever level you want, whether that's vocational training, college, military service or even if you just want to go to work. You need a high school diploma to even apply for any of them," I said. "And, if you want to get your diploma, you need to get it together and take care of business in the classroom."

Toby nodded. Whether he got it or was just sleepy was hard to tell. I sent him back to class and asked the secretary to send in the next one.

Wow. "Find out what you want to do in life and then pursue it." I had been giving this advice for two years.

As I considered the diverging paths of life ahead, I realized that, this time, there were more reasons to go and to do a dozen different things than there were to stay. A week on the trail was all it took to confirm my decision to take on another new challenge: retirement.

The next morning we returned to the trail and, while I finished the final section on this part of the hike, Kate scouted out camping spots near 4 Mile Horse Camp. At the end of the day's hike, instead of heading to a hotel, we turned toward home, to turn in the paperwork that would change the future for us.

Time to mark your progress on your virtual hike on the STS. Go to the URL below to sign the **STS Trail Register**:

www.awalkacrossmichigan.com/
STSTrailRegister

Chapter Eleven

"Many men go fishing all their lives without knowing that it is not fish they are after."

~ Henry David Thoreau

"In every walk with nature one receives far more than he seeks."

~ John Muir

The Other

Most serious hikers hike for the other. The other is what else there is about the hike other than the walking along a path. Let me explain. When you get down to it, one way you can look at hiking is that it's just walking somewhere. Transportation at the base level. Moving from one place to another on foot. You can do the walking part anywhere and, if that was all there was to it, this would just be a book suggesting a particular route to walk. So, really, we should make a distinction here between

...king and hiking. Hiking is different from walking as it suggests a much deeper commitment. A higher level.

Some hikers are not hiking to somewhere but, rather, away from somewhere, something or someone. Putting distance and wilderness between themselves and their challenges provides a cushion to escape the pain, recover from an experience, or salve an open wound. A return to a simpler existence often allows the healing that is needed and can be therapeutic and life-changing.

Life on the trail takes on a rhythm and cadence all its own. A long distance hike develops a routine of its own that becomes the job, the recreation, the diversion and distraction all rolled into one. The rest of the world disappears as you . . . Hike the trail. Hike the trail. Hike the trail. Camp. Eat. Rest. Repeat. Hiking becomes a separate existence that seems to be in a different world, away from the everyday realities.

Hiking at a philosophical level is more than just walking somewhere with a heavy weight attached to your back. Getting back to the basics of what we really require in life --air, water, food, clothing and shelter-- is just part of what makes hiking, especially long-term hiking, so different from walking. Beyond getting back to life at its basest level, it's the journey part that we often miss on the way to the destination, whether it's on a trail or everyday life. It's the learning and experiences we have along the way that make the difference. It's discovering new places, seeing and experiencing things for the first time or re-seeing something in a new way.

But, it's also the struggles and obstacles we face along the way that help to stretch and build us. Famous singer-songwriter Carl Perkins said, "If it weren't for the rocks in its bed, the stream would have no song." The point is that it's what we become as we arrive at the destination as the result of the journey. Being out in nature, hiking in this way, removes the distractions and makes it easier to appreciate what's important. It's clarifying.

So, while it may have appeared, from the vantage point of a casual observer, that I was walking across the state on a path

through the woods, there was more to it t'
simple walk. I was hiking. Life had come to c.
points, where I was consciously aware that I was a
very familiar path, one that I had been on for a very lo.
to chase wildly down another that was unknown, unmarked a.
utterly enchanting.

Sometimes the other is about serious life issues like this. They have deep implications for our lives, for those around us and for the future. It looms up like a monstrous cliff or gigantic wave, threatening to engulf or overwhelm you. But, life is always a potpourri and the other can be any number of things that are lighter and not so serious. For some, just being in nature with the rising and falling tide of seasonal beauty is enough. For others, more concrete and practical activities are the draw, like discovering a new bird to add to the journal, learning about the historical aspects of an area, or gathering mushrooms or other wild foods.

For me, one of the others is often fishing.

Here Fishy, Fishy!

God does not deduct from man's allotted time the hours and days spent in fishing!

~ Epithet of Glenn Campbell Brye

Warning! Fishing Section Begins

The next section of this book may be longer than you care to read because it is about fishing--and I love to fish. If you are not interested in fishing, I'm sorry. I give you permission to read as much as you can stand and then jump ahead. However, if you are a fisherman, then I think you'll probably say that this chapter would be better off being longer. If you're like me, then we shouldn't fish together. Let me explain.

My brother Scott, and I need to take our other brother, Brian, along with us when we fish. My brother Brian is a little OCD not ashamed to admit it. As a pharmacist, that's a good quality to have and people like him are who you want checking to make sure the medications you're taking are not the wrong pills in the right bottle! He will check and double check things, set up systems and processes to make sure that they have been double checked and then worry about whether he has enough safeguards in place to check on the things that need checking. This carries over to his personal life and my other brother and I have great fun messing with his mind by doing little things, like moving the perfectly aligned silverware at his plate off kilter, or sneaking into his bedroom and making a mess out of his perfectly folded sock drawer.

People like Brian love lists and details. They thrive on a schedule. A typical fishing trip with Brian looks like this:

Fishing Trip List

- Motor
- Trolling Motor
- Oars
- Anchor
- Extra Anchor
- Net
- Other net
- Cooler
- Fishing Poles
- Bait -crawlers, minnows, waxworms, marshmallows
- Snacks -jerky, Pringles, Marshmallow Fluff, M&Ms
- Backup net
- Coffee Can (3lb size or larger if you are drinking lots of beverages!)

Early schedule[8]

8:28 – 9:02 Breakfast
9:03 – 9:17 Get boat ready and load car
9:18 – 9:48 Drive to lake
9:49 – 9:59 Launch boat
10:00 – 3:30 Fishing and related activities
3:31 – head back to shore and reverse process replacing breakfast with dinner

Scott and I, being flexible, easy-going souls, are tolerant of Brian's need for this much structure, so we have no problem with this schedule--until we reach 3:31. At that point, if Brian was not with us, we would continue to float around the lake fishing. It is doubtful that either of us would mention returning to land unless:

- A. We run out of bait
- B. We run out of jerky and other manly snacks
- C. Our boat is sinking under the weight from all the fish we've caught

I am sure that you have gathered by now that, if there is one distraction or diversion that I enjoy the most on a hike, it's fishing. If I had gone on this trip by myself, I might still be out there somewhere along a river or a lakeshore with a line and a hook waiting for the next fish story to drag me into the water.

My passion for fishing began early. I grew up three blocks from the Muskegon River as well as close to an abundance of lakes, creeks and small streams. My brothers and I spent hours fishing and I learned how to catch fish mostly by trial and error. Dad introduced us to lake fishing at an early age with cane poles. We would load up the whole family in the station wagon and head out to the public access, where dad would put a bobber on

---

[8] Late Schedule is preferred because fish don't start biting until 11am according to the *Pharmacology Guidebook to Aquatic Craniates*

our lines and bait the hooks. We'd plop them just outside the lily pads where, within seconds, the hungry sunfish, bluegills and perch would attack. In a flurry of frenzied fishing, we would mightily heave them out of the water and onto the gravel parking lot to be unhooked by our parents, our hooks re-baited and the process repeated. We would fish until we either ran out of bait or it got too dark to see. With four boys to tend to, I don't remember either mom or dad with a pole in their hands.

As we got older, we rode our bikes down to the Muskegon River to fish. We could always catch suckers or carp, but also caught walleye, rock bass, northern pike, trout and what we called "shiners." A driver's license gave us the ability to explore farther afield and to fish the lakes and streams all around the county. We expanded our knowledge of fish and their habitats, fishing tactics, fishing strategies and fishing tackle. Fishing continues to be a constant in our lives, though I've come to see that it isn't so much about the fishing as it is the camaraderie and relationships, just like the hiking isn't so much about the walking as it is about the other.

For our nonresident friends along with us, I'd like to point out that the only place other than Michigan you'll find more opportunities for great fishing is heaven. Before you argue for your favorite fishing destination, consider the following facts. In Michigan, fishing is a year-round sport with more than 150 species of fish, thousands of lakes, and miles of high quality rivers. There are fish you catch during the day. There are fish you catch at night. You can fly fish or troll. Jig or cast. The lakes are filled with a variety of big fish as well as small panfish. Rivers teem with trout. Salmon travel from big lakes to rivers. Smelt swarm from the big water to their spawning grounds in rivers and creeks, where you dip them out by the net full. Fish love the state so much that even non-native salt water species, like alewives, migrate through the Welland Channel into the Great Lakes to be where all the cool fish hang out.

Places that you would not normally think of as being known for fishing, like the big cities in Michigan, are places with great fishing opportunities. Detroit, for example, is smack in the middle of great fishing. The Detroit River has a walleye feeding frenzy in the spring that ends when the silver bass are stacked up on top of each other so high that it pushes the walleye into Canada and beyond. Here you go fish catching, not fishing. The Detroit River flows out of Lake St. Claire, just north of Detroit, which is a world-renowned bass fishery. The bass can get big, but the real monsters are Muskies, which you fish for by throwing in lures the size of 2x4's. It's even home to the prehistoric sturgeon.

Whether you like river fishing, lake fishing or what I call "fish hunting"* along small creeks and streams, it's available. You can fish from a big charter boat or a small fishing boat, from a canoe, or any number of places from shore. One of my favorite ways to fish is to silently glide along a river or lake in my **Hobie Pro Angler Kayak**. It's a "sit on top" type of kayak that has been specifically designed for fishing and is equipped with MirageDrive. That's a fancy marketing description for the pedals that power the fins underneath the boat. It allows you to have both hands free and it's a lot like riding a bicycle. Did I mention mine is a sporty yellow?

If you have your own boat, most every town along the shores of the Great Lakes has either a marina or a public access boat launch. One of the items we added to the Brothers' Bucket List is to launch our fishing expeditions from every one of the 1,300+ public boat launches in Michigan, both Lower and Upper Peninsula! That should ensure that we have plenty to do until at least our 90's. Then we'll have to take up another challenge, like playing nine holes on every golf course in the state!

At either end of the STS, there are opportunities to fish the Big Lakes: Huron or Michigan. Charter boats are abundant on both sides of the state and an experienced captain can usually put you on the fish. To find one, start at MichiganCharterBoats[9]. Day or half-day charters are available and vary in price from roughly $300 – $800 dollars. Consider choosing a charter that participates in Michigan Catch & Cook, a new service, started in 2012, that combines two of the best things in the world: fishing and eating. Participating charter boats partner with local restaurants, where they take the fresh catch of their clients to be prepared and served.

There's a dark side, however, to the history of man's dominion over fish in this state. Michigan's incredible fisheries are are not immune to outside influences and the balance required to sustain them are sometimes tipped. The lumber industry, for example, was key in the economic development of Michigan, but it had some negative effects. One victim was the grayling, the namesake of Grayling, Michigan.

It was a strikingly beautiful fish, slate blue in color, sporting a distinctive sail-like dorsal fin. "In the 19th century, northern Michigan's streams literally teemed with them and lore has it that anglers from that time could sometimes catch three fish with one cast. Early historical accounts tell of grayling that 'lay like cordwood in the AuSable.'" Photos from the time period show creels overflowing with fish. Grayling were notoriously easy to catch and were fished commercially to feed the thousands of men in the lumber camps.

While the grayling were feeding the lumberjacks, the lumberjacks were clear cutting the forests, which had a large part in the demise of the grayling. Floating logs to the mills required clearing the waterways of woody debris from the channels and building dams to impound water to be released in spurts to propel logs downstream. The timber scoured the bottoms of the streams, destroying habitat and spawning grounds. In addition, the felling of the tall, shady trees along the banks of the river changed the ecology and the water temperatures rose. The

---

[9] MichiganCharterBoats.com

combination of these changes and the introduction of other more aggressive species of fish were too much for the grayling to survive.

This sad story, however, has some happy in the ending. Lessons learned from the grayling led to conservation practices that have been useful in managing river habitats and other fish populations. The rivers devastated by the lumber industry have recovered and you'll remember from an earlier chapter that the Au Sable River has been recognized as a National Scenic River, designated as a Blue Ribbon Trout Stream and is one of the best brown trout fisheries east of the Rockies. You just won't catch any grayling.

The first third of the STS follows roughly along the Au Sable and the ponds behind the dams not only provide hydroelectric power, but are also outstanding recreational waterways with deep water lake fishing. I was successful fishing from the shore in several places along the river and on the dam ponds. One of my favorite experiences was wandering down to the boat launch dock with my fishing pole at one of the campgrounds on the Alcona Dam Pond, just as the sun was starting to come up. On the third cast I started the day with a 30"+ northern pike.

> **FISHING TIP:**
>
> **I can't tell you how many times my brothers and I have caught fish either heading out into a lake to fish or coming in to the boat launch at the end of a day. Always fish the boat ramp: cast early and fish until you reach shore!**

If the Au Sable was the only fishable water on or near the trail, it would be a worthwhile trip, but that is just the beginning. Strung across the state you will run into a number of other outstanding fisheries that are worthy of being fishing destinations in their own right. They include rivers like the Boardman, the Manistee, and the Pere Marquette. Big lakes like Houghton or Higgins, and smaller ones, like Wakely, Grass, and Lake Dubbonet, are just a few among the many and an additional reason why Michigan is known as the "Great Lake State."

Warning! End of Fishing Section Approaching

Like a buoy on the water that announces your arrival at a dam, waterfall, or other reason to portage, this is a warning that we are nearing the end of the section concerning fishing. I wanted to let you know before we got there to lessen the shock.

In fact, let me end this chapter by telling you that the only place I didn't catch fish on the entire trip was Kneff Lake. It was the campground I had Kate check out for me while I finished hiking the day we left to come home at the halfway point of the hike. The state website that I had found it on said that it was stocked annually with 1,000 trout fingerlings. They either hadn't survived this year, migrated south for the summer, or were impervious to my fishing skills!

Note! End of Fishing Section

This ends the section on fishing. Fishermen should not despair, however, as there are more than a few strategically placed references to fishing in the upcoming chapters to help you make it to the end of the book.

Since Kate and I have returned home to turn in retirement papers, this is a good place for you to also take a short break from the rigors of this vicarious hike. While you're resting, let me entertain you with a news story you may not have seen and some information about one of the most common questions I'm asked: What about bears?

* Fish hunting. One of the techniques we used for fishing on creeks was to sneak quietly up to the bank of a creek or small stream. It was more like hunting because we had discovered that fish in small streams, especially trout, were extremely wary of even shadows on the water. We'd hike along until we found a spot where the creek twisted or there was a bend that created a pool or a place that a big log or rock created a break from the rapids. We learned that fish often held in these positions and watched the stream for food sources floating downstream. We'd toss our lines in above these obstacles or pools and let our bait float into the fish buffet. More often than not, we were rewarded with a fish.

Chapter Twelve

There are lots of ways to die and I am hoping like everyone else to avoid the really horrible ones but, in the end, you only die once anyway so does it really matter how?!

~ Will Swartz

July, 2014. *A lone male hiker was attacked and killed last night in a bizarre encounter when he foolishly tried to hike from one side of Michigan to the other without taking the proper precautions against the dangers lurking in the woods of northern Michigan. The body of hiker, Will Swartz, was found today, badly burned, bitten, bruised, lacerated and contused. "Nearly every inch of him was a mess," said paramedics, who responded to the report of a body found on the Michigan Shore-to-Shore Trail.*

DNR officers have tried to piece together the events of the night and they say their best guess is that the man apparently went to bed covered in clothing that reeked of bacon, crawled into his sleeping bag and fell asleep sometime after midnight. They say his campfire was smoldering and a spark landed on the small wood pile he had constructed next to his tent. The fire spread from the wood pile to the tent and he must have awakened in time to wriggle out of his sleeping bag, in which, the officers say, they found four Eastern Massasauga Rattlesnakes. He then, most likely, shed his clothes to find relief from the Upland Fire Ants that were biting him as a result of inadvertently setting up his tent over one of their nests.

Naked, snakebit and burned, the man desperately ran toward water seeking relief for the bites and burns on over 40% of his body, including both buttocks. As he plunged into the water, he failed to see the safety notice prominently displayed warning that the lake was infested by Michigan Monster Freshwater Leeches. These leeches, an invasive species that can grow to 6 feet long, are attracted by fresh blood and immediately began an attack, attaching themselves all over Mr. Swartz's body. Only his athleticism and strength of character allowed the hiker to stagger out of the water and collapse on shore.

That's where officials say that Will made his tragic last stand, against his final adversary of the unfortunate night. It is rare for the Michigan Woodland Banshee to be drawn out of the isolation it so desperately clings to in the deepest wilderness areas of North America, but, in this case, the sounds of distress and the fact that is was the night of the Summer Solstice, were too much for it to ignore. From the claw marks that shredded much of the skin on the arms and upper torso of the body, it is obvious that this, or a large bear, or several ravenous raccoons, was the most likely assailant that ended the valiant hiker's quest for the sandy beaches of Lake Michigan.

In a final indignity, when officers arrived on the scene, they had to shoot at a pack of crazed chipmunks that were ravaging the body in order to drive them away. The DNR issued a statement assuring prospective hikers of the Michigan Shore-to-Shore Trail that ". . . the trail provides, without reservation, a completely safe environment if the proper precautions are followed, which include an assault rifle, combat knife, pepper spray and a Mommy."

The above gruesome depiction, or a similar version, is the account my loving wife, Kate, was convinced would be the result of my solo wilderness wandering on the STS if I was allowed to pursue hiking it solo. She worries too much. There are very few real dangers in the Michigan woods and they are, in my opinion, a much safer place to be after midnight than most cities. Nevertheless, I sense that you, too, may still have some reservations about how safe you are on this trip with me. To soothe that anxiety, let me share with you my research on the top three Michigan predators we may encounter along the way. I think it will help to ease your apprehension.

Lions and Tigers and Bears, Oh My!

Lions
Panthers leo

Not likely to be seen in northern Michigan. Home territory is Allen Park with regular public appearances at Ford Field during late summer and fall. The Michigan species is often thought by many to be toothless. Beware of their ability to entice fans to watch entire games, where they seem to be hopelessly behind, only to witness them come back to almost not losing in some new and creative way. Rarely seen during playoff season--most have migrated south for the winter golf season.

Oh, come on, that's funny.
Haters, do not email me.
I love watching the Lions!! I just wish they would win the Super Bowl once during my adult lifetime!

Tigers
Panthera tigris

Indigenous to Comerica Park, where their nocturnal prowling is often rewarded by lopsided victories over unsuspecting visiting teams. They have been known to mangle and maul opposing team pitchers and run through the lineup multiple times. Be afraid. Be very, very afraid.

The American Black Bear
Ursus americanus

A frequent question that arises for hikers in northern Michigan is, "What about bears?" One way to respond to that question is to say, "What about sharks? Are we not going to swim in the ocean because you might get attacked by a shark? Sure, there's some risk. But, there's way more chance of being in a car accident or having a plane land on you than being eaten by either a shark or a black bear. I go about my day even though, at any given moment, a meteorite could fall from the sky and squish my sorry self, yes?

I don't mean to make light here of putting ourselves in situations that have some potential risk. I'm not an adrenaline junky looking for my next rush. Quite the contrary, actually. But, when you start thinking of all the things that **could** happen, it would be very easy to go to the dark place and become Mr. Cranky Pants and never go out of the house.

It is true that there are bears in the woods. Actually, there are quite a few bears in the woods. According to the Michigan Department of Natural Resources, "Approximately 15,000 – 19,000 black bears (including cubs) roam the hardwood and conifer forests of northern Michigan. About 90 percent of the bears live in the Upper Peninsula, while the remaining ten percent are mainly found in the northern Lower Peninsula. However, it is becoming increasingly common to see bears in the southern half of the Lower Peninsula."

Wikipedia* reports that there are 96,716 square miles of land in Michigan and roughly two thirds of it are in the Lower Peninsula. If you do the math, that means there are roughly 1500-1900 bears in the entire Lower Peninsula or 1 bear per 20-

25 square miles. True, there is probably a higher concentration of bears in the northern part of the state and still higher populations in wooded areas, but the chances of even seeing a bear are pretty slim when you consider that they are generally not as curious about us as we are about them.

I've seen bears in the wild a handful of times in my life and all have been fleeting encounters with the same result: bear runs away. While I was hiking the STS I did not see a single bear or any signs such as tracks, droppings, claw-marked trees, turned-over rocks, torn-up tree stumps, or broken tree limbs to show that they were present.

In campgrounds or residential areas, signs that a bear has been around are more likely to be tipped over garbage cans, claw marks on coolers or on other food-holding related items, and the destruction of anything a bear might want to get into in order to find food. "They are just a big raccoon," one of the camp hosts I met told me, "and they are more of a nuisance than a danger, if they are around."

Although they are rare, there have been incidents where bears have attacked humans in Michigan. An August, 2013 attack on a 12 year old girl, who was out running in a woodsy area north of Cadillac, MI, got a lot of press coverage. The girl was chased and knocked down twice by a black bear. Deep cuts and gashes on her legs and back required more than 100 stitches. This type of attack is highly unusual because black bears normally shy from human contact.

The Department of Natural Resources says that, "Black bears are shy by nature. If you were hiking through the woods, a bear would most likely hear you or pick up your scent and run off before you even knew it was there." None of the staff at the camp grounds or people I met along the way reported seeing one either. Michigan Trail Riders Association (MTRA) historian, Sally Seaver, said in an interview that, "there have been very few bear sightings and they have never been a problem for our riders."

This isn't meant to say that I don't think there are any black bears on or near the STS. I'm pretty sure there must be, but my experience and the experience of those who know about Michigan bears is that they are not likely to make their presence known unless you surprise them. Most of what's written about black bears in Michigan indicates that you are more likely to see Elvis having lunch in Kalamazoo than to see a bear in the wild. Even so, these are some big animals. Fully grown males can reach 400 pounds and even the little ones have teeth and claws that I don't want munching on me.

"Be prepared," is the Boy Scout motto, so we'll take some precautions when we hike just in case there happens to be a bear or two in the area of the trail. Make a little noise in the brushy areas where we can't see very far. Clean up all food and don't leave any garbage in camp. If we see a bear sleeping, we won't go near it with a pokey stick. And, of course, there will be no sleeping in the tent with slices of bacon on your forehead.

Feel better? I thought so.

MY FAVORITE BEAR JOKES

Two hikers encountered an angry bear and they decided the best thing to do would be to run back to their car.
One of the hikers immediately took off his back pack, sat down and started to take off his boots.
The other hiker asked him what the heck he was doing. Couldn't he see there was a bear coming after them.
The first hiker replied, "Yes, I know. The way I see it is I don't have to outrun the bear. I just have to outrun you, so I'm changing to my running shoes."

~

> Ever go hunting bear?
> Me neither . . . Too cold without clothes.
>
> ~
>
> What do bears call hikers in a tent?
> Dinner
>
> ~
>
> What do bears call a hiker in a sleeping bag?
> Snack in a sack
>
> ~
>
> What do bears call an outhouse?
> A lunch box.
>
> ~
>
> What is the best way to warn bears that you are coming down the trail?
> Wear bells on your shoes.
>
> ~
>
> How do you know if the scat you are looking at is bear scat?
> It has bells in it.

Wow. This has been a really long break from hiking and I'm sure that you're anxious to hear about the incredible adventures on the second half of the hike. It's the part about a murderous park ranger, an island that floats on top of a lake, the famous Volcanic Springs of Mesick, Michigan, hot love on the beach and the triumph of the human spirit. (Actually, . . . now that I think about it, only one of those things is truly in the second half. Also, the one you are thinking it is -- is wrong!)

Sometimes, though, in life, perseverance is necessary to make progress. Take this hike, for example. We started 122.2 miles ago and, by just putting one foot in front of the other over and over again, here we are almost halfway across the state of Michigan.

Think of it. When we began, did you ever think you would make it this far? And yet, here you are. It may help to know that, in a recent unpublished, turbulated study, persevering in hardship has been shown to be a significant factor in building character.

   I'm impressed. So, why are you so set on taking another step and turning the page to the next chapter? What is it that drives you? (You can sit and ponder it a bit, but, really, you should just turn the page now.)

* Wikipedia -- The Encyclopedia Britannica reports that there are only 96,713 square miles of land in Michigan, a discrepancy of three square miles. There are a multitude of very interesting reasons why Wikipedia and Encyclopedia Britannica don't agree, but I'll leave you to pursue them if you are so inclined. Ok, I can't resist. One reason may be that the Wikipedia author was unaware of the 1888 Treaty of Wisconsin, that deeded a three-mile portion of the Upper Peninsula town of Marais to Wisconsin so that the entire town would be in one state instead of divided between the two.

  Some of my librarian colleagues will take me to task here for using Wikipedia as a source, pointing out that, as a librarian, I should model more academically acceptable research standards. They'll point out all of the limitations and risks of relying on it as a credible source. Why, even Wikipedia itself says that anyone who wants to post material can contribute and the expertise of the posters is not even taken into consideration. What you are reading there could well have been written by one of those people (fill in here whatever dull-witted, muttonheaded low-life that comes to mind and is the most offensive to you).

  You could take the approach that our role, as librarians, should be like that of a doctor in advising patients on a diet. Just because something looks tasty and inviting, like a just-out-of-the-oven warm, sugar-coated Krispy Kreme donut, doesn't necessarily mean that you should eat it and expect it to be good for you. No, the uninformed, in this case, need someone to enlighten them and to point out things like the nutritional value of the donut as a snack choice versus, say, a carrot. In the same way, students and those who are unread need to be warned by professionals of the dangers of using unprotected information sources. It's a grave responsibility and one that requires great tact and bedside manner.

I'll respond by pointing out that there is now what amounts to almost a whole sub-genre of blog posts, magazine articles, academic research and other literature devoted to the debate over this. Those who support the use of Wikipedia for information gathering are always quick to point out the same limitations that the anti-Wikipedites do. And then they go on to detail all the merits of the database: articles that are easily understood, contain unbiased and up to date information, good overviews of subjects, vast subject content, information that is easily and freely accessible online, and more.

As librarians, we are trained in evaluating sources for things like accuracy of facts, authority of the author, credibility of the source, bias, objectivity, relevancy, and currency. In the end, we'll all agree that the main objection to Wikipedia stems from the ability of any yokel to edit the material and the inability to prevent malicious misinformation from being foisted upon us.

As a defense for my use of Wikipedia in this case, I'll resist the temptation to respond with, "This is my book and I can darn well use whatever slummy sources that I want to. In fact, I don't even have to resort to finding sources when it so easy to just make stuff up out of thin air, like I did about the Treaty of Wisconsin. Neener. Neener."

Instead, I'll offer up that it was an acceptable source for a non-academic use of information. I'm guessing that every one of our readers knows what Wikipedia is and, further, have used it to quickly look up facts or topics that they are curious about. If this were a scholarly tome written to impress my college grad class professor, I would have chosen something with a bit more dust on it. A writer needs to consider his audience. The fact that I used Wikipedia as a starting point, verified the data with another source, and then reported the discrepancy between them, demonstrates good professional practice and models the acceptable behavior we seek to encourage.

As to the claim that I should model acceptable research standards for students and readers of this book, I'll point out that, in my own subtle way--by using the very source that has been called into question and then raising the question of its accuracy, I have now drawn the reader into an understanding of the pros and cons of the debate and, therefore, done my duty as a librarian to bring issues like this to the forefront. In addition, I've included a bonus demonstration of how easy it is to slip misinformation about a topic into text, i.e. The Treaty of Wisconsin, which sounds perfectly plausible, until you do even a little bit of fact checking and find out there is no town of Marais in either Michigan or Wisconsin. And I'm pretty sure the treaty thing is fiction because I made it up.

I'll rest my defense at this point and humbly ask that my colleagues forgive any perceived misdeed against their sensibilities in this matter. I do so love libraries and would hate to be added to a list of library pariahs and have to resort to slinking into library facilities for the rest of my life.

Chapter Thirteen

"Men do not quit playing because they grow old; they grow old because they quit playing."

~ Oliver Wendell Holmes Sr.

I detest road hiking. It's boring and takes forever to make what seems like progress. There's a scene in the movie, *Monty Python's Holy Grail*, where we see, from the main characters' view, that we are advancing on a castle. The camera cuts away and then back only to have the castle seem farther away. The characters are still moving towards it and the camera cuts away again and then back once more. Still, the castle is no closer than before and may be even a bit farther away. That's what road hiking feels like to me.

    I think my detestment (of course it's a word) goes back to the days of walking with my brothers and friends to middle school. It seemed like such a waste of time. It was roughly 47 miles, as I recall, to get there by foot. Ok, Google Maps says it is 1.2 miles, but I'm sure that the way we walked added some to the distance. That's because we didn't exactly follow straight lines. Our version of the trip wound through the college in our town and even inside several of the campus buildings during the cold weather. It meandered into the party store, the bakery or both and had side trips to explore anything of interest. To amuse ourselves while walking to school we invented games to play. People Tag was, by far, the favorite.

The rules for People Tag were simple:
- ➢ Him with the most points wins.
- ➢ To score a point, him must touch a person other than those that him is walking to school with (this means strangers).

You can imagine what this game looked like from the perspective of an onlooker. A small group of pre-teen boys (we weren't interested in walking with girls yet) is walking down the hall of a college building. Students, staff and faculty (a.k.a., strangers) are walking or standing either singly or in groups along the hallway. They are talking, laughing or quietly preparing for class, unsuspecting of the coming havoc.

Suddenly, him breaks from the herd and, like a Kamikazi dive bomber, swerves left to deftly brush an elbow against the arm of an unsuspecting pedestrian walking in the same direction as the group. Score one point. Another participant makes the same move. Score one point. A third player repeats the action. Score one point. The victim turns around to see what is going on and the rest of the pack dissipates in different directions to seek other targets.

We became pretty adept at playing this game and never tired of the challenge to increase our scores. Swerving across the hallway to touch people coming toward us was difficult, but we managed to act as though we were turning into a classroom or employ some other feint in order to accomplish the feat. We watched in awe one day as Dave Neve scored a double-point by lightly touching a target as he passed by and then, turning around and walking brazenly back toward us, tagged the same target for a two-point. It was a brilliant performance and inspired us to develop even more advanced strategies that involved multi-point and even multi-player combos that made a two-pointer seem rather common (I was going to say pedestrian, but changed it at the last minute to spare you) in comparison. Having a fertile imagination such as this is helpful when road hiking.

Thankfully, there is very little road hiking on the STS, but there is enough to rekindle my detestment (of course it's a word, didn't you see I used it above?). The return to the trail began with an entire day of road hiking and the lucky child to draw the straw to be my chaperone was Jeremy, our middle son, who will tell you that he is the tallest, smartest, most talented, best-looking, etc. (His comments are passionately contested by our other offspring.) Jeremy was eager to join in, even though we were following long, straight stretches along country roads for the day. One of the best ways to make this kind of torment bearable is to have someone along to share the misery. It makes the time pass quickly and the company of my kids is especially enjoyable.

We began after setting up camp and the day began to get hot. I had planned a shorter 8-10 mile loop hike for the day, with the idea that we could get some fishing in when we got back. A bad choice to alter our route resulted in hiking 15+ miles during the hottest part of the day. At this point, I was pretty trail-hardened and used to hiking 10-20 miles per day, even though my feet still hurt. Jeremy, though, was not and suffered some mild dehydration when we ran out of water. We were glad to come to a party store along the highway, where we both bought drinks. (Jeremy later confided that, despite the fact that he had downed two large Gatorades after the hike, he didn't pee until the next evening.) We returned to camp, made a quick dinner and climbed into bed. I was happy to be done with this section of the hike, which was the last one before reaching Grayling.

The halfway point of the STS, Grayling, is a popular stopping point for tourists on their way "up north" in the summer-time.

It's also home to a very unique nautical event, The Au Sable River Canoe Marathon. Tourists and fans, 50K strong, descend upon the town to witness the spectacle, which is held annually during the third week in July. This is not a race for the timid or weak of heart. It covers approximately 120 miles of river, from Grayling all the way to Lake Huron, and takes paddlers just 14-19 hours* to complete as they paddle furiously from start to finish. That's an even longer distance than had taken me more than a week to hike. As an added challenge, the race is held at night! Navigating a narrow, winding river in the darkness of night and avoiding stumps, overhanging branches, and other obstacles is a challenge, even for the professional paddlers that come from around North and Central America.

The race begins in the evening with a LeMans style start, where racers run with their canoes through the streets of Grayling, jump into the river and launch their boats. You can imagine the pandemonium created as 60+ teams of two with their canoes jockey for position in the run and then try to be among the first to get away. Someone always ends up swamping and falling into the shallow water even as the crowd cheers them on.

For more details about the race, the route, events, rules, etc. go to: **Au Sable Canoe Marathon**[10].

Josiah, who concedes the fact that he is almost-the-tallest, but definitely the smartest, most talented, best-looking, youngest son (despite the previous claims of the middle son), arrived early the next morning, as Jeremy and I were fixing breakfast. As a new father with a new job, he had only been able to wrangle a single weekend day and night out of his busy schedule, but he was intent on making the most of it. We had the morning to fish and explore Kneff Lake and, as I previously mentioned, spent a totally unproductive time of it. The boys circled the lake shore casting while I jumped into my float tube, which Jeremy had

---

[10] www.ausablecanoemarathon.org

dutifully brought up to the camp with him. Here we go again, fishing! Just a quick detour, I promise.

Many people are not familiar with float tubes and, even if they are, have not tried fishing from one. A float tube is basically a glorified inner tube. It fits into a nylon jacket that has all kinds of pockets and other features, designed for the convenience of a fisherman. Float tubes are especially handy on smaller lakes and ponds, which are often inaccessible by road, which means that the body of water will probably not have any boats. A picture will make this easier to understand:

Some of my favorite fishing experiences have occurred while peacefully paddling around a small lake or pond in my float tube. North Manitou Island was one of the best. We took the ferry from Leland (more about Leland and Fishtown later) across Lake Michigan to Manitou Island and hiked to Manitou Lake in the middle of the island. So there I was in a float tube, on a lake that was on an island in an even bigger lake, drift fishing as the wind slowly pushed me across the lake. I've seen fishing shows on TV where swordfish or blue marlin leap out of the water, shaking their massive bodies and then crash back into the sea. That's what the first small mouth reminded me of as it cleared the lake 25 feet from me. I caught half a dozen fish in the 25 inch range that day. Each of them tried to outdo the aerial acrobatics of the other.

It was hard to leave Kneff Lake, even though we hadn't caught a single fish, but on this particular day there was a schedule to keep. The next section of the hike was from Goose

Creek to Kalkaska, a distance of 25.3 miles. It was, again, more miles than I wanted to hike in a single day so a halfway camp was necessary. I had spotted several possibilities on the map, but had settled on Camp Tapico, on Grass Lake. I was anxious to get there because my two brothers, Brian and Scott, were joining us for an all-guys weekend of hiking, fishing and just hanging out together.

* Team Triebold-Lajoie are now the 7-time consecutive reigning Champs of the Au Sable River Canoe Marathon, crossing the Oscoda Finish Line in 14:36:18 (14 hours, 36 minutes, 18 seconds).

Kalkaska to Empire Map

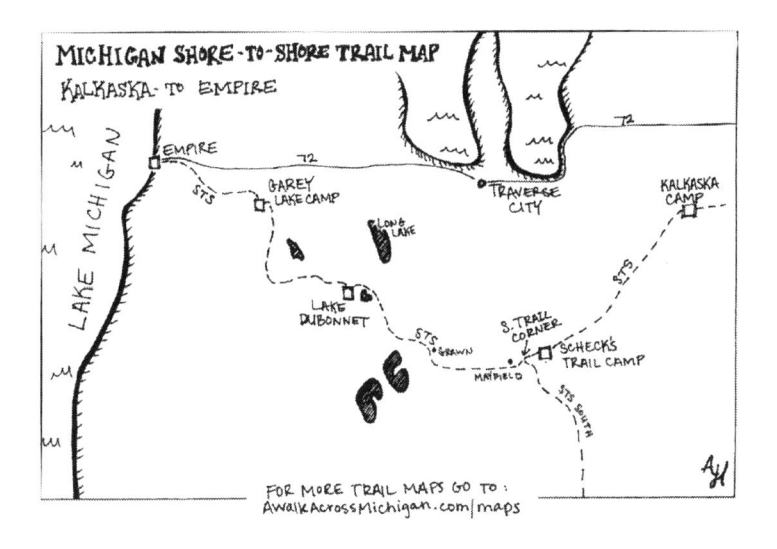

Chapter Fourteen

My brother, Brian, is about the best fisherman in the world - at least that's what he tells us on a regular basis. He rarely uses a rod and reel to fish with, preferring one of several unique methods that he's developed to catch fish.

For example, if it's a particularly hot day, the kind we have in the dog days of Michigan summer, when the heat rises in waves and your bike topples over because the kickstand sinks into the asphalt, Brian will just take a cooler of ice to the boat and motor out into the middle of the lake. "That's where the fish are," he says, "In the deepest part of the water trying to stay cool."

He opens the cooler, stirs the ice up loudly (so the fish can hear it) and then, in one sweeping motion, sticks his head and shoulders over the boat and down into the water. We can hear him saying something to the fish, but to anyone in the boat it just sounds like a gurgled mumbling. Then, the strangest thing happens.

Fish begin leaping out of the water and right into that cooler. We have to fight them off after a while because there are so many in the cooler that it is overflowing. We can see the fish in the water behind the boat following us all the way back to the boat ramp, their sad little eyes displaying their disappointment with the no vacancy sign at the Cold Motel.

It's a strange way to fish, granted, but I've never seen anything more effective on a hot day.

My brothers arrived at the camp before us, around noon, and decided the best way to wait would be to put the boat in the water and do a little fishing. When we arrived, they had already caught some pretty good-sized bass and a lot of pan fish.

Grass Lake is a private lake owned by the Boy Scouts of America at Camp Tapico, northwest of Kalkaska, and is just a short mile off the STS. I was excited to find out more about this camp because my brothers and I all grew up in Scouting. My dad got us started early in Cub Scouts and was our packmaster. We have great memories of the experiences we had in Troop 116, which was sponsored by the Methodist Church we grew up attending. The cool thing was that we went camping all year round, even in the winter months. We learned so much about the outdoors through Scouting as well as developing great character qualities. One of my only regrets in life is being just one merit badge away from being an Eagle Scout and not completing that badge.

When I was planning the trip and looking for potential campgrounds, I spotted Camp Tapico on the map and did a quick online search. What I found was a Boy Scout camp that had cabins and camping spots for rent on the weekends. I made contact by email and, a couple of days later, got a phone call back from one of the scout leaders. He explained that the Boy Scouts had reorganized in Michigan and that a handful of their camps had been closed for the past two years, until they decided what to do with them. Private groups were allowed to rent the cabins and campsites. I told him that I was a former Boy Scout and that I would be backpacking across the state. He gave me the number of the volunteer who was assigned to the camp for that week. I made contact and tentative plans to show up on a Friday afternoon.

Since the entire lake is owned by the Boy Scouts, the only buildings at the lake belong to the camp. It is a wonderful jewel of a lake, with a wooded background, that was a peaceful and tranquil setting for the weekend. It was filled with an abundance of bass, pike, perch, bluegills and other pan fish that seemed ravenous. Perhaps the two year break from being a camp has allowed the fish population to multiply without as much fishing pressure as there would normally be.

One of the unique features of the camp is a group of 10 tree house cabins, built 10-15 feet off the ground. They have the feel of tree forts with the breeze blowing through them and they seem like one of those special, private places we used to search out when we were kids. Although they don't have bathrooms in them, I'm positive the trade off of sleeping up in the air is worth the night time trouble of finding the latrine. My two boys enjoyed them while my brothers and I slept in our more conventional tent.

We had quickly decided on tenting it after we found out that the cabin we had been assigned to was overrun with mice. That important fact was discovered while we were sitting in the screened in porch eating man food (pizza and wings). The advance scouting party of mice showed up to our soiree. They scurried along the edges of the walls and, I'm sure now, that they were just trying to create a diversion so the main army could roll in and devour our feast while we were distracted.

Upon further investigation, we discovered that there was a multitude of mice in the cabin, none of whom seemed intimidated by our presence. The thought of their night time furry foray into our rooms and over us, as we were snugly tucked into our sleeping bags, was not the pleasant nocturnal experience we were hoping for. We quickly moved our sleeping quarters to our tent fortress.

Before you get the wrong idea about Camp Tapico, I should tell you that the camp is not a vermin-infested slum, but well kept up by volunteers who come and stay for a week in exchange for maintaining the property. The cabin we were assigned to had not been used in quite some time and so had become a quiet country retreat for the mouse clan. There are several other buildings used as rentals that are very nice, including the Camp Director's own quarters, that I am confident are pest free. I should also mention here that the Director of the camp had graciously waived the very nominal rental charges when he heard about my hike and about my former Boy Scout membership, so just having a place to pitch our tent was greatly appreciated. If they are still renting cabins out when you read this, I highly recommend spending a night here if you can, especially if you like to fish!

Mayhem Swamp

There is only one section of the trail that I would not care to hike again unless I just wanted to be miserable: Mayhem Swamp. I had seen Mayhem Swamp on both the county map book and on trail maps that we were using and was curious to find out why it had earned such a sinister sounding name. Mayhem conjures up all kinds of possibilities for evil doesn't it?!

My brothers were up for the adventure and, after a breakfast worthy of Swartz men (that means there is lots of food and bacon or other breakfast meats), the three of us set out. Josiah was headed back to his wife and newborn and wouldn't be joining us. Jeremy was not hiking but, instead, had volunteered for Sherpa duty and would meet us at an easy pick up location on U.S. 131 just north of Kalkaska.

Before we enter Mayhem I should warn you by drawing a mental image. Each spring the caribou herds in Canada and

Alaska migrate north to feed during the summer months on the rich grasses of the tundra. If you have seen video of the huge herds running, you know that they look like a living river. What you may not realize is that a desire for a great dinner spot is not the only motivation for the caribou to move so quickly. On their journey, the caribou are frequently plagued by swarms of black flies, mosquitoes and deer flies. They can become maddened by the attacking insects to the point of stampede. That's the picture you should have in your head of the place we are going.

This section of trail, just before Kalkaska, does indeed go through a swamp. There is a narrow two-track lane to follow, so you won't be picking your way neck-deep through snake infested, smelly swamp water if that is what's coming to mind. What you will find is about a mile and half long section of trail where you will be warmly welcomed, as we were, by hungry hordes of mosquitoes and deer flies. Deep in the middle of the swamp, Scott took a picture of brother Brian ahead of him on the trail. On his hat we counted no less than a dozen deer flies. Scott said that in addition to those, there was another cloud of deer flies circling behind Brian as he walked, waiting for their turn to land and to take a ride on his head!

At another point in Mayhem Swamp we were coming up to a small bridge across a creek when the distinctive sound of buzzing wings made us stop in our tracks. It didn't take long to locate the massive bees' nest above us. Looking back from my comfy writer's chair, I'm sure we were more than safe but, at the time, all of those mosquitoes, deer flies and now bees had me rehearsing mentally whether it would be better to jump off the trail into the swamp to roll around in the mud for camouflage or just try and outrun my brothers.

Smack dab in the middle of the swamp we came across a log cabin. It was curious to see because it was obviously being lived in and was very old, though no one seemed to be home. We slowed down just long enough to take a couple of pictures, but wondered why anyone would want to live in the middle of a place where you would rarely be able to enjoy being outside when the weather was nice and where it would be difficult to get to when the weather wasn't nice.

Mayhem Swamp was, undoubtedly, the section of the STS that took the least amount of time to hike. When we cleared the last of it, we found ourselves hiking in a more populated area with houses where the trail followed along power lines and open clearings.

My brothers were chatty that day and the conversation helped cover the miles. We were so involved, in the high level intellectual wrestling of world problems and their obvious solutions that is our normal pattern when we are together, that it was quite some time before we noticed that the MTRA had stopped putting up trail markers at a regular interval. In fact, none of us could remember the last one we saw. We were obviously on the right path because the flat terrain hadn't varied since we left Mayhem Swamp. Everything was good though, because here, right in front of us, was the highway. Cars and trucks were zooming by and this was the pickup spot on the map agreed to with Jeremy.

Cell coverage was strong and I called for our limo driver to come and get us.

"I'm at the pickup spot," said Jeremy, when he called 20 minutes later. "Where are you?"

"We're here!" we told him and described the location from our perspective.

"Well, I'm here and I don't see you."

"Ok. Try driving farther up the road. You can't miss us. We're right on the road."

Five minutes later, still no sign of Jeremy. More back and forth and mild frustration with a son who is, obviously, directionally challenged.

Jeremy diplomatically suggested that we were not in the right place.

"Of course we are! We're here on 131. You're lost!"

To prove it, I dig out my iPad mini with 4g LTE coverage and fire up Map Quest. Sure enough, the little blue blinking dot that shows our location, confirms that we are, indeed, on the highway. It's just that the highway we are on is the wrong highway -- 72 not 131. What we had failed to notice, way back after leaving Mayhem Swamp, is that the power line we were following veered to the left, away from the trail, and headed a few degrees southerly instead of west.

Humbled, but not completely ready to admit it, I informed Jeremy that since he couldn't seem to find us on 131, that we would make it easier for him by moving the pickup spot to a new location, on 72. Ten minutes later we were climbing into the car and I'm sure the grin on his face meant that he knew that I knew he knew what had happened.

Before we send Brian and Scott back to their homes and press on to the next section of the hike, you should know that my brother, Scott, is also about the best fisherman in the world --at least that's what he tells us on a regular basis! Imagine that. Two of the world's best fishermen in the same family!

Not to be outdone by my brother Brian, Scott has also developed some unique methods of fishing without using a pole that he says he learned by living in Ohio. He moved to a small town in a land of the square lakes to attend college, found the woman of his dreams and settled into that strange foreign land.

He married into a farming family and, being a Michigan native, has been forced to endure endless verbal abuse because of the dominance of Michigan athletics over Ohio.

This combination of low geography and farm influence may be part of the explanation for the changes in behavior we have noticed in him over the years. For example, he's developed some lazy speech patterns that make certain words appear to crawl out of his mouth in an unnatural drawl.

Also, farmer Buckeyes in rural Ohio can be a little more creative in their approach to things, which is really a nice way of saying that they can be a bit unhinged at times. I suspect they may all be Cadillackers that couldn't stand the cold, migrated south and settled the area. As evidence, let me tell you about our last fishing trip together.

It was one of those days that Brian had decided to fish conventionally, so he and I were putting our fishing gear into the boat. All Scott put into the boat, besides the cooler of drinks and snacks, was a small backpack and a long handled net.

"Where's yer pole?" I asked curiously.

"Don't need one today," he said in response. "Got somethin' new to try. I learned it from my father-in-law."

When we reached what we thought would be a good place for fish, Scott reached for the backpack. With a mischievous grin on his face he pulled a single stick of dynamite out (all the farmers in Ohio have boxes of this natural resource squirreled away). He quickly lit and tossed it a short distance from the boat before Brian or I could say a word. The water thumped impressively and Scott began netting fish of all sizes and kinds as they swirled up from the bottom of the lake. Brian and I looked at each other, unsure of how to respond.

Finally, in my big brother disapproving tone I asked, "What are you doing?! You can't do that! You're gonna kill somebody --like us!"

"Yeah", Brian joined in, "And, besides, it's illegal!"

Scott looked back and forth at us for a second, reached into the backpack, and pulled out two more sticks of dynamite. He lit them and threw one onto the floor of the boat in front of each of us and said, "Are y'all gonna yap all day or are ya gonna git to fishin'?!"

It's a strange way to fish, granted, but I have to admit that it is thunderously effective!

Chapter Fifteen

I love to be alone. I never found the companion that was so companionable as solitude.

~ Henry David Thoreau

The men's weekend was a rousing success. The departure of the men cleared the way for Kate to rejoin me for a short morning hike with the youngest of our children, Jennifer. Kate assumed her now familiar role of sherpa by dropping Jenny and I off at the trail, just outside Kalkaska, and then she headed for Taco Bell to buy much needed hiking supplies (burritos and other assorted essentials). When lunch was purchased, she drove to the pickup point and began walking back on the trail to meet up with us.

It was a pretty morning for a hike under blues skies that contained a few puffy white clouds. It was nothing like the day that Jen's sister, Noelle, had experienced in the rain, except that we began the day with a hill. I'm pretty sure that within the first 200 yards of each day there was a hill. Trails are like that. They invite you in with a pleasant pastoral scene or beckon to you with the allure of a peaceful path disappearing into a verdant forest. And then, just out of sight around the corner, IT is waiting for you.

It became routine to start out each day wondering how far it would be until I came to my hill. If you have done much hiking, you know that the best and worst thing about a hill is that they are downhill on the other side. The higher it goes up, the lower it goes down. Hard to get up one side, hard to not fall down on the other side.

I have to admit, though, that the hills on the STS are well-meaning and not really what you would call "bad" hills. The worst of them are steep, sandy inclines that leech a little energy as a toll you pay for traveling up them. They aren't like the hardened hoodlum hills on other trails that punish you with bruises and even broken bones on their sharp rockiness. In fact, if you fall on the STS, you'll likely land in a nice cushy pile of sand dune.

Unless you are a birder, you probably don't realize that we've been passing through some pretty rare habitat on this part of the hike. There is a bird, called Kirtland's warbler (Dendroica Kirtlandii), that is among the rarest of the wood warbler (Parulidae) family and it only nests in a few places in Michigan, Wisconsin and Ontario. The same "pine band" that was responsible for the logging era in Michigan is the same habitat where the Kirtland warbler takes up residence.

The Kirtland spends four months of the year in this northern habitat and then migrates south to spend the winter months in places like the Bahamas, Turks, Caicos, and Hispaniola Islands. It eats the typical bird diet of insects, but it also likes ripe blueberries. With the amazing number of blueberries growing along the trail, it's a wonder they are able to fly south when it's time to go.

The Kirtland's warbler is a finicky bird that has the personality of a two-year-old. It will only nest under the branches of jack pine trees that are 5-20 years old. The jack pines must be living. Oh, and they prefer stands of the trees that are over 80 acres in size. There should be ". . . dense clumps of trees interspersed with numerous small, grassy openings, sedges, ferns, and low shrubs." Each breeding pair wants 6-10 acres to call home, but, if the conditions are ideal, they can get by with an acre and a half. Sheesh.

Life is good for the Kirtland's warbler. Spending the summer months at the northern getaway. Eating blueberries until you can just barely fly. Hanging out in the jack pine condo. Catching the jet stream south before the polar vortex descends. Basking on the sunny Bahamian beaches. Yes, life is good, except for the cowbirds.

The brown headed cowbird (molothrus ater) was also called the "buffalo bird" because it traveled with the bison herds on the plains, feasting on the insects that followed the herds. Their vagabond lifestyle following the herd resulted in a peculiar behavior when it came time to nest. Instead of building its own nest, the cowbird lays eggs in the nests of other birds, where they are fed and raised by the adopted parents. The clear cut logging of the Michigan timber forests gave the cowbirds new territory and the Kirtland's warbler was an ideal candidate for the surrogate egg strategy.

If Kirtland's warblers are two-year-olds, cowbirds are the four-year-old bully at preschool. Cowbirds hatch earlier than most birds and are aggressive. They compete with later hatchlings for food and the best seat in front of the TV. "Studies have revealed that, when one cowbird egg is laid in a warbler nest, only one to three warbler chicks may survive. If two cowbird eggs are laid and hatched in a warbler's nest, none of the warbler chicks survive. Heavy cowbird parasitism is believed to have been a major factor in the decline of the Kirtland's warbler population."

The cowbirds might have wiped out the Kirtland's warbler in Michigan if it weren't for a coordinated effort, beginning in 1972, by the U.S. Fish and Wildlife Service, the USDA Forest Service, Michigan Department of Natural Resources and the

Michigan Audubon Society. They began an aggressive effort to trap cowbirds in the nesting areas of the Kirtland's warbler. This effort successfully curtailed the number of cowbirds. Today, they carry on the work started in the 70's by continuing to trap the rascally cowbirds. In addition, this group of agencies manage the lumbering activity in the nesting area and oversee controlled burns, replanting and other conservation practices. The result has been a growth in the nesting pairs of warblers.

For more information about Kirtland's warbler, A 2013 Michigan Notable Award book, *The Kirtland's Warbler*, by William Rapai, is an interesting account of the bird's discovery, natural history and controversy.

And here we are, hiking on hallowed warbler ground.

Jen and I talked on and off as we hiked, but I don't remember much about the conversation on the trail from that day or with any of the others that I traveled with for that matter. As a father, I've learned that it isn't necessarily the words that are the most important, although you do need to say them --things like, "I love you," "I'm proud of you," and, "You want a piercing where?!" No, it's not so much the words that are remembered, but the shared experience of doing something special together that creates the bond. That specialness is enhanced in nature.

It seemed like Jen and I had hardly been hiking for anytime when we met Kate coming down the trail. We trekked back to the car and had a Taco Bell buffet for lunch. When we were done, I gathered all the leftovers and a couple of burritos and stashed them in my backpack for an easy, no-cook, no-dishes dinner. As much as I didn't want to say good-bye to Kate and Jen, I was anxious to push on to the next stop, Guernsey Lake.

This is the part of the story where you need to remember that fictional newspaper article at the beginning of Chapter 12. You know, the one about my gruesome demise by the mangy hordes that are waiting to attack any solo hiker who ventures into the wilderness, because this is the part of the hike where I do just that. I had hiked with Kate, all but one of our kids, my brothers, and my brother-in-law and his sons. Now, I had purposely set aside the next five day section of the trail to do solely on my own.

I assured Kate that I was well prepared, would call her every night, and that the life insurance was in good order. She reluctantly agreed to turn me loose into the scary woods after wrangling a promise that I would carry pepper spray for the bears. I didn't tell her that I thought that if a bear was going to eat me he would prefer that I was carrying a stick of butter rather than some peppery seasoning that would make him sneeze.

We said our good-byes. Kate and Jen were on their way back home and I was on my way to five days at the casino. Typo here. Should read "five days of adventure on the trail." Please correct and delete "at the casino" before final publication. I had about 10 miles to hike to Guernsey Lake and made it easily in plenty of time to set up camp and enjoy my Burrito Supreme before it got dark and the beasties came out to get me. Well, "easily" may not be the best word choice since I now had a 45 pound pack to carry. Just for reference sake, that's five pounds over the weight limit Spirit Air imposes on their customers for the privilege of checking a suitcase to fly in the cold cargo hold. That weight overage, by the way, will cost you an additional $25, added to the $21 you paid to check a bag when you bought your ticket online. If you didn't pay for it online, there are more charges.

I'm not complaining here about having to carry 45 pounds with me --I wanted everything in that pack. I'm just trying to help the non-hikers among us envision what that weight looks like in terms they can relate to. Lash a 45 pound suitcase to your back and try to do anything you normally do during the day and I doubt that "easily" will be one of the descriptive words you select for the experience. The only thing that will come easily after hauling 45 pounds of stuff around on your back for hours is sleep at the end of the day and that's exactly what I did on my first night alone in the wilderness.

The night passed without incident and I woke with the sun in the early morning. The hike to the next camp, Scheck's, was a shorter one of only 10-12 miles, so I took my time getting started. Breakfast was a fine meal of gourmet oatmeal with brown sugar, dried Michigan cherries, and powdered milk. Some wild blueberries were the perfect addition and a protein power bar provided a turbo boost of energy food to fuel the morning walk. Hiking by yourself means that you are right on time for everything and late only if you say so. A couple of hours later I proved it by departing right on schedule. I spent the entire day without seeing another human being on another part of the STS that was mostly in the woods.

I arrived at Scheck's Horse Camp in the late afternoon and was unsurprised to find that it was totally empty. The problem is that the pump for water in many of the horse camps requires a generator. Those are really heavy so I hadn't brought mine along. The camp was on the Boardman River so I could filter water if nothing else was available. There was a little water left in my supply, but I decided to hike on the road around the camp to see if there might be another source for water nearby.

Just down the road from Scheck's Horse Camp was a State Forest campground, with a hand pump and a single pickup camper inhabiting the entire park. It looked like a peaceful, quiet, pretty place to stay right beside the river. I pitched my tent and set up camp for the night. A peaceful end to the day disappeared an hour later when a YMCA bus arrived and dumped out 30 fourth and fifth grade girls, their gear and three teenage counselors for an overnight campout. The possibility for solitude was gone, but the entertainment had arrived.

One group, consisting of what seemed to be the smallest girls of the party, was assigned the task of filling everyone's canteens, by pumping water from the hand pump across from my site. They attacked the chore with enthusiastic glee. The long, squeaky handle of the mechanism required the combined strength of two of the small girls to leverage water from the ground. First, it took seven or eight pumps of the handle to raise the water to the faucet and then a continued effort to make the water flow in a steady stream. Unfortunately, a dozen pumps were all a pair of the girls was able to manage before they needed to call in another duo for relief. Whenever the girls switched places, the priming would be lost and the operation would begin again. It took almost half an hour to fill their water bottles and canteens. Yes, I know I could have helped them and I did think about it, but I was busy boiling water for dinner and they were having as good a time with their chore as I was having as a spectator.

On another front, the girls chattered and giggled as they tried with varying degrees of success to turn piles of nylon and poles into shelters that they could sleep in. Muddles of 3-5 girls would attack a pile together. Two girls would hold up the tent fabric and the others would stab at the support loops with the long, elastic-connected telescopic poles, while they all simultaneously offered enthusiastic encouragement and conflicting directional advice. When a habitable structure did not appear from their workings, they would pull everything apart and restart the process.

I watched with amusement because I, too, have experienced the frustration of trying to set up outdoor shelters advertised as "easy assembly," with color-coded poles and grommet holes that don't seem to have the faintest chance of meeting together to form anything remotely resembling a tent. The matching rainfly would seem to be better employed as a blanket rather than expending the effort to attach it as prescribed in the long ago lost directions. The counselors, however, were competent and, as they visited each group of girls, a small tent city was soon erected and the even more entertaining task of creating dinner for the now hungry throng began.

While I dined on a fine freeze-dried Chicken Teriyaki, I watched the party. They were roasting, burning, dropping and gobbling hot dogs and chips washed down by cups of camp bug juice. Later, a dessert of s'mores turned into an impromptu marshmallow fight that exploded into a chasing, pelting mob that lost interest in wild rumpussing only when the marshmallow supply was exhausted. This was not exactly the tranquil wilderness experience I had expected on this part of the journey, but it was an amusing diversion.

Camp songs around a bright fire followed and, when the lullabies were all done, the festivities moved to smaller gatherings inside tents, where flashlights shone on tent walls and quiet secrets were exchanged. It was moonlit and late before the last of the babbling brook of conversation faded into dreams and serenity finally reigned.

The YMCA bus returned mid-morning the next day and the girls, their gear and their counselors boarded and disappeared for fun in some other location. Just as quickly as calm returns after a tornado passes through, the camp serenity returned, with tranquil chirping of birds and other muted woodland rustlings. I passed another enjoyable day hiking around the area, fishing, reading and resting. A second night was undisturbed by any further camp outings, but the stars that night were all the entertainment I needed. The netting on the roof of my tent was almost transparent and I fell asleep watching the night sky.

Chapter Sixteen

"A bad cup of coffee is better than no coffee at all."

~ David Lynch

The next day began like most other days on the trail, with stiff stretching of sore limbs and reluctant wriggling from cozy comforts. A peek through the tent flaps revealed another perfect summer day that was just beginning on our side of the world. Strange that others, twelve hours away, were preparing to end the day. Hazy light was dull on the newly formed dew. I dressed quickly and began preparations, even in the wild, to soothe my morning addiction.

I came to appreciate the hold that coffee can have on a person when I was on a father-son camping trip with a friend (who shall remain nameless here--though Mark will recognize himself in the story-- for fear of shaming him in public). I woke up one morning to the sound of my friend making a fire and rattling some pots as he heated water. When I came out of the tent he was carefully pouring steamy water over a sock draped over a camp cup. The sock had coffee grounds nested in it and the water was slowly steeping and draining through the sock where it was collected on the other side. Who does that? Why would someone drink coffee strained through a sock? I didn't ask any questions about the sock, though, because I didn't want to know. He lovingly coddled the cup like it held liquid gold. Desperate. The epitome of desperation. This was before I became a coffee lover. I should have heeded the warning signs to stay away from the stuff. I now understand.

I've evolved into a coffee snob. It was a slow descent into the world of caffeine-infused beverages.

Black.
Grande. Venti.
Normal.
Caramel macchiato.
Cafe con leche.
Cowboy coffee.
Espresso shots.
Cafe mocha.
Iced coffee.
Cappuccino.
Frappuccino.
Caffe latte.
Not hazelnut.
French press.
Turkish coffee.
Fresh-ground.
Whole beans.
Grind your own beans.
Keurig.
Dessert coffee.
With cream. With flavored creamers. Flavored syrups. *Not hazelnut.*
With spirits.
Mixed blends.

Gevalia.

Jamaica Blue Mountain Estates, Hawaiian Kona, Ethiopian, Kenyan.

Cafe Bustelo, Maxwell House, Folger's, Yuban.

Tim Horton's, Bigby's, Dunkin Donuts, Starbuck's, Caribou Coffee, Seattle's Best.

So many more.

Freeze-dried crystals.

Instant coffee.

Motel coffee.

Waiting room coffee.

Gas station coffee.

Vending machine coffee.

Not hazelnut.

I could go on, but you get the picture.

Curious, too, since I didn't become a regular coffee drinker until well into my teaching career, though I grew up in a household where my parents and every adult around me consumed potfuls of the stuff everyday. A recent article about how to roast your own coffee beans using an air popper, the kind you use to make popcorn, caught my attention just before leaving on this trip. The author claims that it produces coffee that is as much improved over whole beans roasted and packaged in air tight pouches as fresh ground beans are from beans that are pre-ground. It's only a matter of time and a good hot air popper sale away.

Not that I have a particularly discriminating palate when it comes to coffee. It mostly tastes the same to me and I drink it several ways. Black is good, especially in the morning or with desserts in the fuzzy, mind-blowing sweetness range. I can add creamer, plain or flavored (not hazelnut), and drink it with or without something to eat with it. I learned to love cafe con leche, which is Spanish for "coffee with milk," while living in Mexico. The milk is scalded, which gives it a unique flavor, and a cup of cafe con leche with a tamale in the mercado (market) in the morning was a favorite. It differs from the French cafe au lait, which is also, "coffee with milk." There are slight differences among these and the other ways to drink coffee, but it's those subtle differences that make a great cup of comfort or a bitter ending to the story. It's the same obsession that wine aficionados, craft beer lovers and cigar smokers have with their vices; the search for the perfect combination of strength, temperature and taste.

There are several ways to make coffee on the trail but, for a decent cup of coffee without a lot of hassle, I go to one of two proven strategies. Whenever we travel and stay at motels, I always snag the single cup coffee pods and pouches in our room and stick them in my luggage to take home, where they are transferred to the camping box. Hot water in a camp cup and a coffee pod will do it. A little more elaborate method is to use the Aeropress Coffee and Espresso Maker I discovered in Tim Ferris's book, *The 4 Hour Chef.* It makes one of the best cups of coffee you will ever have.

P.S. If you find yourself in a situation where you are truly desperate, you can always try the sock method!

No doubt all this talk about hot, caffeinated beverages has the coffee fanatics among us pouring a fresh cup to enjoy as we head out on the trail. You'll need the energy boost today because it's 25.2 miles from Scheck's to Lake Dubonnet, also known as Mud Lake. Don't despair about the distance, though, because there's a nice surprise waiting. Before we depart and while you're enjoying that cup of java, let's take a quick Pure Michigan Tourism commercial break and learn about a couple of crops that grow just as prolifically as blueberries do along the trail.

The Michigan Department of Tourism runs some incredibly effective advertising campaigns, like the Tim Allen narrated Pure Michigan ads, that attract thousands of visitors to Michigan each year. Forbes named Pure Michigan one of the All-time 10 Best Tourism Promotion Campaigns Worldwide. Tim admits that the

Pure Michigan ads he makes are some of his best work and he's a proud Michigander. There are a couple of his best about the Traverse City and Grand Traverse Region, which is only a dozen or so miles south of where we'll be passing today. To see the videos go to: **Pure Michigan**[11].

All of the accolades for this region of the state are not without good reasons. Traverse City enjoys a reputation as one of the finest places to visit, not only for its natural beauty, great summer climate and outdoor activities, but also for food and drink. It has gained national and international attention from magazines like *Bon Appetite*, which listed it in 2012 as one of America's Top Five Foodie Towns, *MidWest Living*, which named it among its Five Top Food Towns, and *National Geographic*, which named it one of the best summer trips of 2012. Famous chef, Mario Batali, owns a former trout camp on the the Leelanau Peninsula and often shares his favorite local establishments on *Mario recommends*[12].

Among the many fascinating stories about this area is that of Peter Dougherty, a Presbyterian minister. He moved to the Traverse City area 160 years ago and the Indians he lived with called him, "Mickoos" (little beaver), because he did "a heap lot of work for his size." In 1852 he decided to plant a cherry orchard even though the prevailing opinion was that cherries would not grow so far north. It turns out that all the sand we've been trudging through is great soil for growing cherries and that Lake Michigan tempers the cold, Arctic wind during winter and cools the hot summer temperatures to provide the perfect growing environment. The orchard thrived. Today, Traverse City is the Cherry Capital of the world, producing 70-75% of the nation's tart cherry harvest and 20% of the sweet crop.

The plentiful crops of cherries led to the creation of one of the largest festivals in Michigan, the annual National Cherry

---

[11] Awalkacrossmichigan.com/Puremichigan

[12] http://www.mariobatali.com/michigan-summer/

Festival. Since the first Cherry Festival, held in 1926, the Cherry Festival has grown to include a parade, car and truck shows, fireworks, airshows and fabulous food and drink featuring, of course, cherries. There's a National Cherry Queen competition. Half a million people attend over the eight day celebration held during the second week of July. The Festival advertises that 85% of the events are free and that it's very family friendly with activities that include arts and crafts, turtle races, sand castle building, etc. It has been named one of *USA Today*'s top ten annual festivals.

The same environment that is great for growing cherries is also ideal for grapes. A thriving wine industry has grown up in the Traverse City area. Wine tours are a favorite activity and trips to the many vineyards and tasting rooms might be something you want to try when we finish the hike. For the out-of-staters with us, don't miss exploring this area!

The trail didn't even attempt to camouflage the starting hill of the day with the customary 100 yards of flat easy terrain to lull me into unawareness. Instead, it stretched up right away with a sandy incline off the access road to the trailhead before settling into the more gentle rolling terrain that is more typical of the trail. My pack settled into the grooves it had carved in my shoulders and I loped along in a determined stride.

Woods and fields. Woods and fields. Woods and fields.

Sometimes all you do is walk and think and just be.

After a morning hike of about seven miles, I came out of the woods into a neighborhood on the outskirts of a small place on the map called Mayfield. I hiked by the houses and was delighted to find Mayfield Country Store: a grocery, hardware, party store, gas station, restaurant-deli combination on a busy highway corner. An establishment that had quaint written all over it. It's the kind of outpost you find in lots of small Northern Michigan villages. They serve the locals by providing a little of everything you might need right now and don't want to have to travel to the next big town to get. You can pick up a part to fix your toilet, grab a gallon of milk and a loaf of bread, buy a fishing lure, get gas for the truck, have a snack and take something home for dinner all at the same place.

When I opened the door and entered, a horse's neighing played out over the store speaker system announcing my arrival to those inside. About a dozen different sound effects rotate through the playlist and each time the door opens, a new one plays. The store had a small diner area with home cooked breakfast items on the menu that tempted me, but it was the smell of pizza coming from the front deli counter that won me over. I devoured two slices and had a brownie for dessert with another cup of coffee.

While I was there, I learned that Mayfield has the distinction of being the home of the Adams fly, which to fly fishermen, is one of the most famous flies ever created. You can visit the original pond and river where the fly was tested and feel the historical significance oozing over you as you stand on the bank that harbored such an auspicious happening.

I was excited about Mayfield for a different reason, however.

The STS turns into a looong section of road hiking at Mayfield -- 10-12 miles of road hiking. And, you know how we hate that, right? Well, the good news is that Jamie Jo Isanhart, my niece, lives in Grawn, Michigan, which is only ten minutes from Mayfield. She and her husband, Mark, provided an oasis in exactly the right spot. Mark picked me up and gave me a ride that leapfrogged me to the next campground at Lake Dubonnet (also known as Mud Lake).

Lake Dubonnet is a unique lake. It was formed from Big and Little Mud Lakes when a dam was erected between the two. The water that flows out of it becomes the Platte River and thousands of fishermen, canoeists, kayakers and, especially, tubers enjoy riding on its back, until it leisurely empties into Lake Michigan, almost 30 miles away.

It's a flickering blue and green jewel set in a surrounding of green that's not far from Traverse City, but has the feel of being in a much more remote place than it is. Loons on the lake fill the air with their haunting call and, just when you feel like you could be the only one around for a 100 miles, a float plane drops out of the sky and makes a landing run. It taxis to a stop, turns, then powers up and takes off again, headed back to the base for the seaplane flight training school in Traverse City. The lake is a good practice spot for future bush pilots.

There's another reason, I found out after I returned home, that Lake Dubonnet is unique. It has a floating island. No kidding. It supposedly moves several hundred feet each year. There aren't any signs pointing out the island; no Tikki Bar commercializing the whole thing with outdoor patio seating and Lake Dubonnet Floating Island souvenir mugs. Although I had heard somewhere about the famous floating islands in Titticaca, it was a new subject for me and my Spidey sense said it could be a hoax, like the **Tree Octopus**[13] I had tried to purchased online. Perhaps someone was selling lake front lots. I turned on my librarian superpowers.

A Google search for "floating islands" will return, "About 4,640,000 results (0.31 seconds)," if you want to wade through that kind of nonsense. To appease my librarian friends, I skipped the Wikipedia entry and went right to the hard stuff. There's a wonderful online reference source provided by the Library of Michigan that you might try the next time you need information. It's called the *Michigan ELibrary*[14] and it's filled with many databases and sources that are credible. You will find that a search for "floating islands" on Mel will return hits from a variety of sources and a mention of the Uros people of Peru, who make their home in Lake Titicaca, is inevitable. They live on what are really floating rafts of reeds. I added a visit to Peru to the bucket list and moved on.

---

[13] http://zapatopi.net/treeoctopus/
[14] http://mel.org/

Two fascinating books surfaced (sorry, I couldn't resist!) on the subject of floating islands and both had mentions of Lake Dubonnet:

Floating Islands: A Global Bibliography, by Chet Van Duzer ". . . is a unique treasury of information about one of nature's marvels: floating islands. Its bibliography contains more than 1,500 citations of books and articles in 20 languages on the subject. The entries are annotated and cross-referenced, and there are both thematic and geographic indices. All aspects of floating islands are addressed."

It turns out that there are, indeed, floating islands, both man-made as well as naturally occurring and there seems to be an abundance of them located around the world.

Floating Islands: An Activity Book, by Richard Heggen, is a brand new 2015 eBook offering that adds a playful, thematic narrative to the subject and I found sections of it intriguing. For example, Lake Dubonnet's floating island is noted, in a chapter on the physics of floating islands, as having the record for the tallest trees recorded. There's a physics discussion about torque and wind pressure against the mass of the trees and the island's tipping point. Heggen quotes a Traverse City Record-Eagle Newspaper story from November 16, 1970:

"Grand Traverse County's floating island still is wandering around its water highway, Lake Dubonnet, southwest of Long Lake and north of Interlochen . . . Originally two acres in size, the floating island has dwindled in area, but still supports tamaracks and other trees reaching heights of 60 feet and diameters of 12 inches at the stump."

A search for the Traverse City Record-Eagle Newspaper archives revealed that they aren't available online that far back but I was really interested in the story. The Traverse Area District Library was listed as the holder of the records. I called the reference desk and, within minutes, Katheryn had a full page copy of the paper and a clipping of the article on its way to me by email. Gotta love librarians. You should add one to your team!

The story has a picture of the floating island, which had moved to within 50 feet of the boat launch at the lake. It confirmed, from a Department of Natural Resources spokesman, that ". . . The island came into being when two lakes, still shown on many maps as Big and Little Mud, merged in 1956 in a conservation project."

As I was thanking Katheryn for her excellent service, she said that she didn't believe the island was still there. Naturally occurring floating islands do have a tendency to diminish in size over time and it is common for them to reattach to the shore. I added a return visit to the lake (of course I'll have to bring a boat and fishing rod) to see for myself. Those strange, watery noises I heard out in the lake late at night may have been an island sneaking around when it thought no one was looking.

There are two campgrounds at Lake Dubonnet. One is the MTRA horse camp and the other is a State Forest primitive camp. The deciding factor for me was the boat ramp at the State Forest site. A bonus was the realization that I could use this camp as a base and not have to carry a backpack again. In addition, Kate would be rejoining me here in another day to finish the trip. The final surprise of the day, though, was the best.

The weather was that perfect Michigan 75 degrees and sunny. Now, Mark and my niece Jamie are busy young parents, with a business that keeps them focused on working long hours, but Mark seemed as ready for a break as I was. When he saw the boat ramp, he mentioned that this would be a great place to bring his family and boat, which he hadn't used all summer, for an evening picnic and fishing trip. It was an easy sale to close. Four hours later, Mark and Jamie returned, with four kids and a boat in tow. Best of all, after so many days of eating freeze-dried food and oatmeal packets, they brought along one of the best hot, steamy, cheesy, meaty, tasty pizzas I've ever had.

We had a great time fishing and Xander, their youngest blonde-haired imp who had never caught a fish before, saw the bobber bob and felt the first addictive tugs of a fish on the other end of a line. He heaved mightily and, not only was the fish hooked . . . so was Xander!

Chapter Seventeen

"You will never reach your destination if you stop and throw stones at every dog that barks."

~ Winston Churchill

Tomorrow's hike will be a long one for us. I wanted to warn you, so you can get a good night's rest and be ready for an early start in the morning. This is a good place, as we get ready to make the last pushes to Lake Michigan, for one final fascinating story about Michigan's past that most people know very little about.

A few miles north of where the STS ends in Empire, MI is a little village called Leland, where we'll visit a place called Fishtown. It's a collection of gray, weathered-wood fishing shanties and old icehouses that have been converted to shops. The site was designated an Historic Place in the National Register of Historic Places in 1975 and it is being preserved as a link to the maritime history of Michigan.

Fishing has a lot to do with the history of this place. It's built on the site of an Old Ottawa Indian fishing camp on the Carp River, now the Leland River. The 15 foot drop from Lake

Leelanau to Lake Michigan created a natural fish ladder that made the site attractive to white settlers, who established a settlement in the 1830's.

The town is crowded as we drive into the village on a tree-lined two-lane road that dissects the village. An expanded parking area in the marina still begs for more room as pedestrians and cars intermingle in the close quarters. Two fish tugs, that still operate a commercial fishery, float gently at the long docks overhanging the Leland river and campers, awaiting the ferry to North and South Manitou Islands, watch as the fishermen unload their daily catch. The wood-smokers behind Carlson's Fish Market fill the air with the wonderful wood-fired aroma of smoked fish. A crowd of visitors bustle in and out of the screen doors to purchase smoked salmon, white fish, lake trout and other fresh fish.

You might think, with all this talk about fishing, that we're about to explore the fishing industry in Michigan, because you know how I love to talk about fishing. It's tempting, for sure. There was, after all, a commercial fishery in Fishtown as early as 1880. Trout and whitefish were plentiful and the fishermen and the group of shanties they built at the site to process their fish and service their boats have a long and interesting history. Their lives were filled with stories of big catches, narrow escapes and tragedies at sea, tales of camaraderie, heartbreak and joy.

There are so many interesting things we could learn about Michigan fishing, like the harrowing story of how the commercial fishing industry in Leland and all over Michigan almost perished in the 1960's. Overfishing and sea lampreys had driven native lake trout to extinction in Lake Michigan and they were almost gone in Lake Huron. The populations of whitefish were at a low point. Millions of dead, stinking, invasive alewives washed ashore on the Lake Michigan beaches and because of it tourism all along the shore was in decline.

I guess the story of Howard Tanner's decision, as the state fisheries chief in 1964, to stock 658,760 one and a half year-old salmon smolts on the Platte River and Bear creek will have to wait for another day, even though it spawned (sorry) a totally new sport fishing industry that erupted when the river-spawning salmon returned three years later.

It was so successful that "Shoreline communities later complained they had been unprepared for the onslaught of fishermen that converged on their communities in the first years of what would be an explosion of salmon. There were not enough boat launches, parking areas or public bathrooms. They ran out of Flatfish (lures), they ran out of gasoline, and then they ran out of beer and they were really in trouble. . . There were so many boats on Platte Bay you could just about walk on them."

It's troubling to leave this story, though, because most people think salmon were introduced to solve the problem of all the dead alewives on the beach and that's a myth. The fact is that the alewives were just following the typical pattern of invasive species. That is, they explode into an environment where there are no checks on their population growth, reach a peak, level out and then decline. Coincidentally, they hit that peak in 1967 and died off just as the salmon returned. It appeared that the salmon were the heroes when in reality they just happened to be there. We really wouldn't want to leave people believing such a misconception like that.

It's also hard not to mention stories like the encounter teenager William Gauthier had with the Leelanau Lake Monster in 1910. He was perch fishing in a shallow part of the lake, filled with stumps and dead cedar trees sticking up out of the water. He chose what he thought was a five foot tree to tie his boat up to and got the shock of his life when his rope touched the tree-- and two eyes opened! I guess you'll have to read the rest of the story on your own at:

http://awalkacrossmichigan.com/stories

No, if we're going to get to the really fascinating story here, we can't spend time talking about fishing. We don't even really have time to learn about a very unique non-profit organization, aptly named the Fishtown Preservation Society, that purchased the fishing shanties of the historic village in Leland and two fish tugs. The Society is the driving force behind the efforts to preserve a little slice of a place that matters. You can read more about it at:

http://awalkacrossmichigan.com/fishtownmi.org

I really shouldn't take the time to tell you, either, about one of Kate's favorite stores at Fishtown, the Dam Candy Store. Whenever we're anywhere near Fishtown, say Detroit or even Toledo, she gets a kick out of saying stuff like:
- "Can we drive up to that Dam Store town and go to the Dam Store?"
- "I'd really like to go to Fishtown and sit outside that Dam Store and have some Dam candy."
- "I wonder if that Dam Candy Store has any Dam candy."
- "Gimme some Damn Candy!" -- sometimes she just forgets!

If Kate was in charge of naming the shops in Fishtown there would be the Dam TShirt Store, the Dam Cheese Store, the Dam Smoked Fish Store and, of course, a general store named, The Dam Store with products like Dam Mugs, Dam Key Chains, Dam coasters, etc.

Oh, that reminds me. You don't know that there's a dam on the river at Leland and that's the reason there's a Dam Store there. For candy. Sorry, I should have mentioned that Antoine Manseau Sr. and John L. Miller built a dam on the Carp River in 1854. The dam created one large lake, Lake Leelanau, out of what was originally three smaller lakes. The Michigan lumber rush was in full swing then and the backwater allowed logs from the surrounding forests to be floated along the shore down to a saw mill next to the dam.

The original dam washed away and was rebuilt several times over the years. Leland Power and Light Company, which was eventually purchased by Consumers Power, (remember the brothers Foote from Chapter 5?) built a concrete monster of a dam that was blown up in 1908 by angry farmers. They were mad about losing several thousand acres of farm land by the encroaching water. Tough crowd. I'm sure there's an interesting story there, but we can't dawdle here.

Nor do we have space to devote to the intriguing history of how this little village remade itself over and over again. Fishing was always a constant in the village but it, too, went through several changes to its present state today. It evolved from subsistence fishing to mostly commercial fishing to mostly sport fishing in response to government regulation, invasive species, changes in the fish ecology and the introduction of salmon.

If you visited Leland at different points in its history, you would have had difficulty recognizing it as the same place. The building of the dams mentioned above gave birth to the lumber industry and their saws buzzed through the timber changing the face of the land. Leland Lake Superior Iron Co. did a makeover of the village when it fired up an iron smelter from 1870-1884 that gave the area a grimy industrial look. Leland returned once again to lumbering and producing shingles after the iron company went bankrupt, transforming it again.

Michigan lumbering was on its way out at the end of the 1800's so, during the early 1900's, Leland tried out a new identity as a summer resort. The area was discovered by the wealthy in cities like Chicago, who came by Lake Michigan passenger steamers to vacation on the beautiful shores of Lake Michigan. They built summer cottages. Hotels, resorts, restaurants, shops and all those fabulous summer memories followed and tourism took center stage.

All of these things about fishing, lumbering, and Fishtown are interesting, but they're pretty easy to find out about. Googling terms like, "Michigan salmon fishing," "alewives in Michigan," or even, "Great Lakes shipwrecks," which we haven't even talked about, will keep you engrossed for hours. A trip to your local library will give you a list of great items to read on any of those topics, and more. You'll even find some specific books, like Michigan Notable Book, *Leland, Michigan's Historic Fishery Fishtown*, by Laurie Kay Sommers. It has stories of the people, historical photos and lots more about Leland and Fishtown.

You could do that on your own, but I made it easier for you by selecting some of the best informational sources about all of those topics and more at:

http://Awalkacrossmichigan.com/resources

"So, Will. What is the fascinating story you want to tell us about Michigan?"

I'm glad you asked. I thought we'd never get to it.

Chapter Eighteen

"If a man does not keep pace with his companions, perhaps it is because he hears a different drummer. Let him step to the music he hears, however measured or far away."

~ Henry David Thoreau

When we were doing the virtual walk-through of Fishtown, did you notice the icehouses? Most people don't. They were used to store large blocks of ice that were cut from lakes, ponds and rivers. Ice houses disappeared with the ice trade, but during the last part of the 1800's and into the 1930's they were commonplace. By 1930 Fishtown had five ice houses. Today, only two former ice houses survive: the Ice House and the Warren Price Shanty, currently known as the Hall Shanty, which originally had an ice house in the east half of the building.

Ice houses were simple buildings, usually wood-framed, that didn't have windows or doors, but did have openings at the top to provide light and ventilation. Access ladders ran up the wall next to slat-covered openings from the ground to the roof. The walls were filled with sawdust for insulation and a well built ice house could keep ice through the hot summer months and even into the next season.

When I saw the ice houses it reminded me of something I read a long time ago by Henry David Thoreau. You noticed, didn't you, that a lot of the chapters in this book begin with a quote from Thoreau? Most of them are from **Walden** and I remember the first time I read it. It was memorable because I was sitting in the back of Mrs. Altenburg's eighth grade English class.

One of my friends, Mark, had tied a long, blonde hair that he gotten from Julie, the girl in front of him, to a fly he caught. He held one end of the "hair leash" between his thumb and forefinger and the fly was making long, circular loops above his desk. When Mrs. Altenburg could no longer ignore the snickering and suppressed giggling, she came to investigate.

"You let that go!" She commanded. Mark complied and the fly, burdened by the weight of the hair, strained slowly across the center of the room and out the door into the hallway. The class was totally disrupted. Mark got a complimentary visit to the principal's office.

Normally, I would have been one of the snorters cheering Mark on, but I wasn't paying any attention because I was engrossed in the story of a guy living out in the woods. Thoreau built a cabin on Walden Pond, where he lived for a little over two years, and wrote about the experiences he had pursuing a simpler life.

. One morning, during the winter of 1846-47, Henry woke up to the sounds of "a hundred Irishmen, with Yankee overseers, came from Cambridge"out on Walden Pond. They had come to "get out the ice. . . with many carloads of ungainly-looking farming tools--sleds, plows, drill-barrows, turf-knives, spades, saws, and rakes." The account that follows describes the process of harvesting ice from the lake and it's a process and industry that only our elders have any recollection of.

Even in Fishtown, where ice was still harvested from Lake Leelanau and Lake Michigan for years after refrigerators and freezers were available, there is little evidence of an industry that was once commonplace. An ice machine was finally installed in 1960 and, as the ice houses became unnecessary, they were eventually repurposed as shops. The annual ice harvest that drew the fishing community together disappeared.

A new community event on the ice has arisen, however, called "berging." It's a unique activity that takes place when the ice is thick enough to support a crowd of people and it's a cross between a tailgate party and a river cruise. When the ice has frozen to a safe enough thickness, a crowd gathers on the edge of Lake Leelanau. Chainsaws bite through the ice, cutting a large slab free from the lake, and an iceberg is born. The participants load up the floating platform with their lawn chairs, coolers, grills, picnic gear and the spirit of people who know how to have fun.

It's a leisurely hour and a half float trip down the river to the dam and another special memory is made in a place that is already unforgettable for those who visit. **The Leland Report**[15], "an online diary of life in the Leelanau Peninsula for those who just can't get enough," provides a daily report in words and pictures of this event and others.

The ice trade in Michigan was a massive industry because Michigan has the two most important commodities for ice: cold winters and lots of water. In addition, much of the ice in Michigan was accessible along shipping routes. Although harvesting ice developed later than on the east coast, Michigan became a major source of ice and it was prized for its clear, clean purity.

---

[15] http://lelandreport.com

Harvesting ice was often a cold and dangerous source of work for the thousands of men who came to work during the winter months on the Great Lakes and other inland lakes, rivers and ponds in Michigan. The process involved scraping the snow off the ice and sawing large cakes or blocks that were loaded onto horse drawn wagons and taken to ice houses. They were unloaded and packed in layers using sawdust for insulation and, in Michigan, many of the lumber mills had ice houses right next door, taking advantage of the sawdust they produced.

Ice was delivered to houses on routes, two or three times a week, like the ones milkmen had to deliver dairy products. Customers had subscriptions and put up a card in the window letting the ice man know how many pounds to leave. Ice boxes were a standard household item. A tin-lined box on top held a block of ice and a separate compartment below held racks for food. They were messy contraptions requiring regularly emptying a drain pan on the bottom.

The entire ice industry--thousands of jobs, new tools and inventions, the introduction of a luxury that most kings in the past were not able to enjoy--all of it, was started by one man, Fredric Tudor. Here's the short version of the story.

Like many of the Internet startup whiz-kid founders of our generation, Fredric Tudor was a 22 year-old that ". . . marched to the beat of a different drummer." He had an idea and he had the passion to take great risks to see it come into being. He decided against a Harvard education in order to pursue what the Boston business community and society thought of as a crazy scheme to cut ice out of a pond on his father's farm, load it onto ships and sell it to people in faraway tropical places.

It was such an out of the box idea that no ship owners were willing to take on his ice cargo and Fredric ended up purchasing his own ship, in 1806, in order to start the enterprise. When his brig, *Favorite*, sailed on February 10, 1806, it had 130 tons of ice on board. The Boston Gazette posted: "No joke. A vessel with a cargo of ice has cleared out from this port for Martinique. We hope this will not prove to be a slippery speculation."

The ridicule didn't deter him even when it appeared that his critics were right. Much of his first cargo melted during the three weeks it took to sail south and there was no icehouse at Martinique to store the cargo when it got there. Although he was still able to sell a good deal of ice in Martinique, the venture suffered a significant loss.

Fredric regrouped and the following year he shipped 240 tons of ice to Havana. Once again he lost money and it wasn't the last of his problems. The Embargo Act of 1807 prevented him from shipping to Havana. He lost cargoes, faced massive debt, was sued by his creditors and spent time in debtor's prison. The War of 1812 crippled his shipping of ice. He suffered a bout of depression. Each obstacle only served as an experience to learn and to adapt.

He set up agents to manage the business in foreign countries, opened new markets, negotiated monopoly contracts to be the only supplier of ice, built ice houses in the ports he shipped to, experimented with various insulation materials and worked on designs for insulated cargo areas on ships and in ice houses. After years of struggle and persistence, Fredric finally began to see some fruits from his labors. He sent a cargo of ice to India and the British welcomed him with open arms, even building ice houses for him. His business became profitable and over the course of the 20 years it took to establish it, Fredric paid off all of his massive debt and was a millionaire at the time of his death in 1864.

For the history buffs among us, there are two resources that will provide lots more on the subject. *The Frozen-Water Trade*, by

Gavin Weightman has the whole intriguing story of Fredric Tudor. For the real hard core historians, a trip to *Knowlton's Ice Museum*[16], in Port Huron, Michigan, is in order. It's dedicated to chronicling this industry and preserving the tools of the trade.

---

[16] www.knowltonsicemuseum.org

Chapter Nineteen

Are you awake?"

"Yeah."

"We need to get up and get going."

"Yeah, I know."

"You're not moving. Are you going to get up?"

"Sure. Give me a minute."

"Well, I'm just sayin' we have a long way to go and we should get started."

"Ok."

"Are you ready to get up yet?"

Silence.

"Did you go back to sleep?!"

No response.

"Ok. I didn't want to do this, but you leave me no choice."

"Oh, man! ---I have to pee soooo bad! I'm up! I'm up already!"

There are days when you hike that the miles seem effortless. They just drift easily by and you arrive, almost magically, at the end of the trail. This will not be one of them.

"Three more minutes at base pace and then we'll get started." Christine, my trainer, smiled and start-ed her stop watch. The workouts at Orangetheory Fitness[17] are intense. It's sixty minutes of heart-rate monitored, interval training that's been my regimen two to three times a week for a little over a year. "Base pace" is a comfortable speed that you can, supposedly, keep up on the treadmill for a very long time. On the flat screen monitor above the treadmills, I watch my heart rate climb into the green band and level out at 78%. My body would rather do almost anything other than run, even at a "comfortable" speed.

There are days when you hike that the miles are more difficult. They stretch endlessly on and on. You feel as though you've been transformed somehow into the mythical figure, Sisyphus, and are never . . . ever . . . going to be able to drag your pack up the next hill. When you somehow . . . finally . . . do . . . reach the top--there's another hill.

"Ok," said Christine, "For this next 5 minute block, I want joggers and runners to start at a six percent incline at your base pace. Every minute we'll add one percent to the incline and I want you to stay at base pace. For the last minute we'll go all out." The short, lithe, female body next to me serenely pounds out the pace at a furious rate, as I struggle to keep up at half her speed. My heart rate climbs through the orange level and into the red. Five minutes later it begins to drop as we "walk it out" for a short recovery period.

Orange is the new fit. "Backed by the science of post-exercise oxygen consumption (EPOC), heart-rate monitored training is designed to keep heart rates in a target zone that spikes metabolism and increases energy. The result is the Orange Effect

---

[17] http://awalkacrossmichigan.com/Orangetheoryfitness

– more energy, visible toning and extra fat and calorie burn for up to 36 hours after your workout!"

Some days it's a struggle to even get started.

"Transition time. Cardio team head to the floor area. Floor team head to the treads." Christine was still smiling as I traded my space in Cardio Hell for an equally torturous piece of real estate in Core Workout Hell.

"This next block is all about endurance. High reps with low weight. First exercise, hammer curls into an overhead press. Slow and under control. Work those muscles. Second exercise, tricep dips. Back against the bench. Lower your body slowly and press up with your arms. Third exercise, Burpees. (Burpees. Why did it have to be burpees? I hate burpees!) Three exercises. Fifteen reps. Twelve minutes. You should get through all three exercises three to four times each. Ready? Three, two, one, go!"

I glanced to the right. Lithe-body girl was lifting bread sticks with apples on the end posing as weights. I hefted 35 pound real-man builders. Small consolation, knowing that tomorrow the muscles doing the work today would struggle to lift a pillow to make the bed.

The map says that it's 18 miles between Lake Dubonnet and Gary Lake, the final camp on the STS and then another 9.2 miles to Lake Michigan for a total of only 27.2 miles left. Like a horse nearing the barn, I'm eager to get there. To make up for some of the road miles skipped the day before by catching a ride with Mark, I'm adding part of the Lost Lake Pathway. It's a loop trail that starts and ends at Lake Dubonnet. I grab a slice of leftover pizza and pair it with oatmeal for a satisfying, if not gourmet caliber, start to the day. Of all the days on the trail, this will be the longest and most challenging physically.

There's a point in every hike where I want to quit.

Actually, there are several and I've come to recognize them as frequent visitors to my mind. At the first thought of, "I need to get up and get started," a group of perfectly acceptable excuses attach themselves, like preschoolers clinging to my legs:

"You need a little more rest."

"That blister on your heel needs a bandaid."

"Your water filter needs to be cleaned out."

"First, you really should eat something so you have some energy," followed immediately after I've eaten by, "Not really a good idea to hike on a full stomach."

When I refuse to entertain the excuse troop and get moving, it's not long until the Frenchman, Miner DesComforte, pulls alongside and engages me. "You ave such a beautiful and brilliant mind. Surely, zer iz somezing zat you would rather be doing outside of zees woods."

The natural beauty of the world around me is enough to dismiss the intruder and it's usually quite some time before I notice long time friends, I.B. Weary and U.R. Fatigued, have sidled up silently beside me. They generally travel along at my pace, whining about this tough incline we're going up or remarking on how hot it's suddenly gotten. Sometimes they tug insistently on my sleeve when a comfortable spot to sit comes into view.

The most annoying visitor, however, is WWE star, X. "Hoss" Chion. He's a madman and his favorite ploy is to rush up on you shouting, "Stop! Stop!" His clamorous message urgently promises that superstar WWE wrestler, **IMMINENT DEATH**, is on his way and will be here any second. He never shows up.

I make good progress during the morning, only stopping for short breaks, but late afternoon arrives and I'm still miles from Garey Lake, where Kate is going to pick me up. I've lost track of where I am on the map. I.B. Weary and friend, Fatigue, have shown up when I finally come to a wooden sign on the trail that someone has posted. Cruelly, it reads, "Only 4 More Miles." Later, I learned that it was an inside joke of the MTRA riders, who, in response to the question many newbie riders ask, "How much further is it?" always responded with, "Just four more miles!"

Trainers say, "Listen to your body." Most of what mine tells me to do is quit. I've learned to ignore most of what it says. Exercise and workouts follow this same pattern and, if you think about it, so does life.

The last four miles are what I call Zombie Land hiking. It's the one foot in front of another, just keep going and don't stop because if you stop I'm not gonna get up again unless some world catastrophe starts with a volcano spewing out from underneath where I'm sitting kind of hiking. I'm relieved when Garey Lake finally comes into view. I drag through the camp which is, of course, uninhabited and park my weary self under the sign at the entrance to wait for Kate. I look but, once again, **DEATH** has not shown up.

A short while later, we're on our way to dinner and back to camp.

Are you sleeping yet?
No.
Why not?
I'm too tired to sleep.
Do you want to go for a walk?
No! Are you nuts? I've been walking all day!
Well, I'm just sayin' you might want to go for a walk in a couple minutes is all.
Why would I want to do that? Can you just shut up and let me rest?
Ok. But don't say I didn't try to warn you.
Warn me? Warn me about whaaa ..... Oh crap! Now I have to go pee!

Chapter Twenty

I left the woods for as good a reason as I went there. Perhaps it seemed to me that I had several more lives to live and could not spare any more time for that one.

~ Henry David Thoreau

The final day of the STS was bittersweet, as are many endings in life. I was certainly glad to be done with sleeping on the ground, which has no chance of competing with the cozy comfort of our Sleep Number® Bed. The final five days had been more physically taxing, but I also felt refreshed emotionally from the time on my own. It was sad, though, to think that tomorrow I would wake up in my own bed instead of in the woods somewhere. There was the satisfaction of finishing a longer hike but, when you accomplish a goal, it's not long until the little mouse of a question comes creeping into your mind and asks, "Ok, what's next?" And that little vermin was already scratching!

I was glad that the last day was a shorter day so that we would have some time to spend at the beach. The 9.2 miles took less than two and a half hours, even though I tried to walk at a pace slower than the mall walk speed that my feet were demanding. This was the last day and I wanted to savor the journey, not rush past it like some sale-crazed shopper.

The trail section from Garey Lake to Empire begins with a long, straight trail through the woods that crosses some roads and fields. Then, it abruptly cuts up and onto an elevated, long abandoned railway bed that is one of the prettiest walks on the trail, just before it pops out onto the highway leading into Empire. It was on this section that my now familiar daily deer sighting ended with a perfect record. The honorary three member color guard made a final appearance and gave me a symbolic farewell with a white tail salute. Or else they ran off to find some River Deer buddies to tell them where I was!

The final three miles follow along Highway 675 and it's not bad, as road hiking goes, because the trail is just off the road and mostly tree-lined. It was warm and sunny, again. I was grateful for the shade. Traffic whizzed by and I imagined the cars were loaded with excited vacationers headed for the same Lake Michigan beach I intended to reach today. A mile down the road, a curious sight slowly crept into view.

There was a field on the other side of the road that had rows of telephone poles stuck into the ground, some of which were on an angle, that made them look as if they had been thrown into the ground by some giant javelin thrower. Thick wire was tautly strung between them to make a massive trellis and something vine-like was growing up it. My first thought was grapevines, but it wasn't like any vineyard I had ever seen before. I crossed the road to get a closer look.

They were hops. Michigan has a booming craft beer industry and the growth of all things that support the industry, like growing hops, has been along for the ride. According to the Michigan Brewer's Guild, "In terms of overall number of breweries, microbreweries and brewpubs, Michigan ranks #5 in the nation – thus supporting its claim as "The Great Beer State." Later I learned that there are a dozen or more craft breweries just in Traverse City and the surrounding area. It seems a perfect complement to the wineries and distilleries in the area.

Hops are interesting crops. They are the female flower or seed cone that grows on a perennial, vine-like plant. Hops come from the same plant family as cannabis and, inside the cone, are tiny yellow sacs that contain the good stuff, acids and essential oils, that beer makers use. Hops are the bitter that balance the sweetness of malt in beer. Depending on the variety, they can add bitterness and flavors like grass, herbal, citrus, pine, spice and others. In addition, they have antiseptic and preservative qualities and are also what builds and holds the head of foam on a glass of beer when it is poured.

Most of the world's hops are, overwhelmingly, used to produce beer, but there are a couple of other uses. Nonalcoholic sodas, for example, are produced with hops. Malta is popular in Latin America and Julmust is a traditional Christmas beverage consumed mainly in Sweden. There is also a small market for hops in herbal medicine as a treatment for restlessness, anxiety and sleeplessness. A popular folk remedy for insomnia is to make a pillow out of hops.

There are hundreds of varieties of hops and they grow in several parts of the world, but it was unusual to be looking at a hops farm on a road in northern Michigan. Over 90% of commercially-grown American hops are produced in the Pacific Northwest states of Idaho, Oregon and Washington. The Yakima Valley, in Washington, is famous for its hops and alone produces 74% of all American hops.

Growing hops takes some serious investment in time and money, especially for startups. The 18-foot trellises are expensive and a hops farmer needs drying equipment and big-boy toys, like trucks, tractors and other massive pieces of customized machinery. The machinery can sit idle for up to 10 months of the year if that is the only crop.

A hops "field," "yard" or "garden," as they are commonly called, is a giant trellis that takes 5,000-7,000 feet of cable per acre to build. The trellis needs to be strong as there are more than 1,700 strings of hops hanging from it per acre and the strings can produce up to 2,000 pounds of hops.

Hops season begins in the spring and the work is intense. The hops plants come out of dormancy and this is where the plant can be a little needy, like a finicky puppy. They are pruned and then trained to climb up the wire by wrapping some of the bines (the tendrils of the vines) around the trellis at just the right time during a three week window. Too early and it results in as much as a 40% lower production of hops. Too late, similar result. Once they begin to grow, in perfect conditions, hops can grow up to three feet per day.

Harvesting hops begins in late August and, depending on the weather and the variety of hop, goes on into early October. The vines are cut about 3 feet above the ground as well as at the overhead support wire and then loaded onto a trailer. They need to be processed quickly or they lose the properties that make good beer. Each string of hops is fed into a machine that strips the leaves and vines away. Then they are taken to the kiln, where they are dried for approximately nine hours. After a 24 hour cooling off period, they are compressed into pellets, baled, wrapped in burlap and put into cold storage warehouses.

Hops journey from the warehouse to the mash of a beer brew and the making of beer is part science, part art and a lot of creativity. Beer makers use hops at various points in the process of making their brew to add more or less bitterness and to add the variety of flavors that the different types of hops have. The reason you may like one beer over another has a lot to do with the hops.

To celebrate all this "hoppyness" and to celebrate the fact that you have vicariously hiked with me across the entire state of Michigan, I think this is an appropriate place for a toast. We only have a couple of miles left on this journey together and I want to thank you for coming along. Just down the road a little bit, in Bellaire, MI, is Short's Brewing Company, where I'd like to introduce you to the craft beer world.

Every brewing company has a story and Short's is a saga of overcoming the challenges that many entrepreneurs and business startups face. Joe Short, at age 22, registered Short's Brewing Company as a Michigan business in 2002 and ". . . Words cannot describe the heartache, stress, losses, physical and mental fatigue, and great rewards experienced throughout the struggle to bring the Short's Brewing Company project to fruition."

You can read the story at: **Short's**[18].

Today, Short's vision is to be an establishment that is not only a destination for craft brew enthusiasts but is also like the American colonial pub. The pub was unique in early America as a pillar of the local community. It was a social gathering place to catch up on daily happenings, meet with family and friends, and enjoy a meal or fresh brewed beer together. What better place to meet and raise a glass?

For my beverage, I'm having one of my new favorites, a Short's Local's American Lager. I think it's a great choice for this occasion:

"Local's is a perfect beer for the seasoned craft brew enthusiast and someone new to microbrews. When Short's first opened, there was not a great deal of craft beer available in the area. Joe Short wanted to create a beer that would appeal to new craft beer drinkers who lived in Michigan and would introduce them to the complex flavors of other beer styles. Local's is a light yet very tasty lager. The light pilsen malt creates a soft and subtle flavor profile that finishes crisp and clean on your palate."

---

[18] https://www.shortsbrewing.com/about/our-story

SHORT'S BREW
LOCAL'S
AMERICAN LAGER
Your neighbor knows where it's at

My toast these days is a simple one: "Endless Summer!"

I was ending the hike in the same manner that it had started. I crossed the highway and hiked into the downtown section of Empire heading for the big water finish line. No waving crowds. No bands playing. No big welcoming party. No trail markers. They end about a mile out of town. Except for the water pack and trail clothing I was wearing, no one would have known that I wasn't just out for a leisurely stroll through the village instead of completing a 19 day hike across the state.

Kate had returned to camp to perform the last of her Sherpa duties by packing up our camp and wasn't due to meet me yet. I sat on a rock wall and waited at the entrance to the park so that we could take the last few steps of this journey together. I thought about all that had happened in my life during the past year.

I had turned 60. A respectable human milestone. Halfway as I like to say. Five kids. All grown and raised. All married. All gainfully employed (no one living in my basement). Healthy. Financially stable. Still married to the love of my life. Grateful for so many blessings. Life is good.

My final year in education had been filled with both challenges and rewards and I felt good about leaving on my own terms. It certainly felt like the 28 years in education had flown by. I was a little sad, however, knowing that I would miss working with the many good friends I had made over the years. Some of them, I knew, would only hear bits and pieces of my life and they might assume I had gone over the deep end if they heard bits of news from any of the great adventures I was embarking on. Walking across the state was just the beginning of what I had planned.

I had regained my vision. For the past couple of years, a cataract had been forming in my good eye. I had poor vision in one eye already due to multiple eye surgeries, a dozen years ago, for a retinal detachment. Now the cataract had gotten bad enough that I could no longer follow a golf ball off the tee nor track a racquetball while playing. In March, I had the cataract removed and my vision went from dim and clouded to crystal clear 20-20, literally overnight. Those who have had similar experiences will know the joy I felt.

I had also gained a clear vision of what I wanted for my life as I began a new one. Thoreau said of his decision to leave Walden Pond: "I left the woods for as good a reason as I went to them. Perhaps it seemed to me that I had several more lives to live, and could not spare any more time for that one." I was leaving education early and retiring so that, like Thoreau, I could get about living more than one life--hopefully several more. Like the current generation, I was going to remake myself, do a makeover, revitalize, rejuvenate, regenerate, retool and reboot.

One of my models for the Third Act is Chris Crowley, author of *Younger Next Year* and *Thinner Next Year*. He is an author and retired lawyer, rides his bike on 100 mile jaunts, skis double diamond hills and is basically a physical fitness nut who advocates working out six days a week and eating stuff that's good for you. Did I mention he's 80? He's still on a mission, though, to inspire people to adopt healthy, vibrant lifestyles that are all about using your gifts and being as heavily involved in living this life as possible. Kindred spirit.

In a recent email newsletter he gave some savvy advice from the vantage point he has, 20 years ahead of me: "My instinct at this point: Give it the old Wiley E. Coyote: Chase that roadrunner a hundred miles an hour till I go off the cliff. Look down. See ya." Nice to have a like-minded soul like Chris blazing the trail ahead.

It had, indeed, lived up to being the start of an epic year.

When Kate arrived and parked the car, I dropped my backpack and gear and we headed down to the beach for a final photo shoot. The beach crowd was just coming to life and I was a little self conscious about taking pictures in such a public place.

The frigid water of Lake Michigan, even in August, can take your breath away. It's the main reason that shipwreck survivors in the Great Lakes, especially Lake Superior, are so few in number. The cold is refreshing, though, and is one of the reasons why we love It. Today, it was sunny and Michigan gorgeous at the beach and I was ready to celebrate more than just ending a walk across the state. I had indelibly marked the commencement of a new decade and a new chapter in life. I waded into the water and washed the grime of five days and nights away. That moment was exactly the way I had envisioned finishing the hike, even before taking the first step on the Michigan Shore-to-Shore Trail.

My solitary trek was at an end.

> *The storm, which had ravaged the woods and mauled my soul, dissipated in a long dripping that lasted for a gray-filled night. As morning light filtered it's fingers through the tall trees, I unwound myself from the twisted tangle of underbrush, where I had fallen and, mercifully, lapsed into dreamless sleep. The dark tunnel of undergrowth, thick and thorny, cut and caught on bare skin, trying to hold back my inevitable progress into the light. I emerged loudly from the woods, a newborn soul, one newly conscious of it's own existence.*

Peace was, once again.

You Did It! You Made It From Lake Huron To Lake Michigan On A Virtual Hike With Will!

Sign the trail register and I'll send you a memento!

Michigan Shore-to-Shore Trail Register

www.awalkacrossmichigan.com/
STSTrailRegister

Epilogue

"Everything good takes time and it takes time to be a writer, but by Gad I'm going to be one some day."

~ Ernest Hemingway

This is my first book. When I started the project, it was just something on my list of things to do. You know, one of those bucket list of items we all have. Quite often it's a list that never gets done and is stuffed with items like:

- Learn to speak German
- Play the piano
- Develop six-pack abs
- Visit Fiji
- Trace my family genealogy back to Noah
- Do something to help end hunger and promote world peace

I don't think I was very different from a lot of people who want to write. I really didn't care if anyone read my book. Didn't care if anyone liked it. Didn't care if it made any money. I was interested in writing because I like to write. It's therapeutic. It's a creative outlet. Writing a book was just a big item waiting for a check mark on my life list and, being newly retired, it seemed that I might have the time to devote to it.

My goals have changed since I began writing. One of my guiding mantras is, "How you do anything is how you do everything." I do care, greatly, about this book. I would like people to read it. I hope they like it. It would be nice to make some money from it, so Kate doesn't have to get another job to support the lifestyle I love and have grown accustomed to.

I've learned a lot about writing, the publishing process and book marketing from this project. According to those who make lots of money at book writing and publishing these days, the first step is to determine your market. I didn't. If you really want to sell lots of books, the best markets are: Romance (think *50 Shades of Grey*), Teen Dystopian Fiction (think *Hunger Games*), Horror (anything by Stephen King & Co.), or Mystery/Thriller (Grafton, Christie, Forsyth, etc.). I suppose I could make revisions to make *A Walk Across Michigan* fit in one of those genres, but it would be a wholly different book in each case!

The next step is to create a product that meets a need. Well, maybe. Actually, I'm learning that the market I want to appeal to is bigger than just 60 year-old guys like me that suddenly get an urge to carry their belongings on their backs across Michigan. Writers and books are a lot like food. Not everyone likes spicy, hot Mexican or Thai food, but most have, undoubtedly, found a favorite food or dish of some kind. Similarly, not everyone will enjoy reading *Harry Potter*, by J.K. Rowling or *Game of Thrones*, by J.R.R. Martin, but there are books and authors that they might admire or they would if they knew about them.

If someone says, "I don't like to read," chances are good that they just haven't discovered that they like pizza. Mixed metaphor, sure. But the point is this: just as there are a variety of cuisines to meet the variety of culinary tastes, so there are a variety of authors and books to meet the variety of tastes of readers. Like all writers, I'm hoping there are readers out there who will like what I cook up, will share it with others and will want more.

I have no doubt that my editor's advice to, ". . . put the book away for six months and then take it out again and read it," would result in some more rewriting and polishing that would, ultimately, improve this effort a bit. Balanced against that advice, however, is the counsel from the other side of the fence, that at some point you just have to call it good enough and publish. Add to that a bucket list that is growing like a weed mainlining Miracle-Gro and the scale is tipped.

So, here it is.

Lots of people have written books. There have been times when I've wandered up and down the aisles of a library or book store and marveled at the sheer collective volume of written words. I've thought about how long it would take me to try and read even a grain of sand's worth of what's on the shelf and realized I can't get to all of them. Not only that, but I am amazed at the prolific nature of some individual writers, who have been able to produce such a staggering stable of thoroughbred works.

And the flood of new books continues at a massive rate. Bowker reports that over one million (1,052,803) were published in the U.S. in 2009. In addition, there are too many to count in the years before that and six more years' worth added to the catalog, competing with my offering for your attention. So, I am not a little humbled to have managed, finally, a single volume to add to man's collected works. I'm grateful that you chose to pick up and read this book out of all that prodigiousness.

The fact that you have this book in your hand means that I have crossed off #1 on my bucket list, which was to write a book. It also means that my market is, at least, one more larger than just family and friends who don't wish to see me starve or move in with them! If you truly liked this book, I'm flattered. I'm hoping that this is a good point, while you're still mesmerized by whatever good feelings you have toward me and to this work, to ask for your help.

I'm not some big time author with a massive budget and an army of marketing minions to do the fancy book descriptions, set up signings, or arrange interviews on talk shows to market my writing. I have to do all that stuff on my own and that's where you come in. There are a couple of things you can do to help me promote this book and the other ones I haven't even thought up yet. It won't cost you anything and I've done most of the work for you. I promise it will only take a few minutes of your time and I'll be extremely grateful. You can help me out at: **Help Will**[19].

Paddle to the Sea, by Holling C. Holling, was one of my boyhood favorites. It's the story of a young Indian boy who carves a little man in a 12-inch canoe that he names Paddle-to-the Sea. He sets the canoe off on a journey from the snowy banks of a river on the Canadian side of Lake Superior and it travels through the Great Lakes, the St. Lawrence River and finally the Atlantic Ocean.

Along the way there are dangers and adventures and each time Paddle-to-the-Sea appears to have come to the end of his voyage, a kind stranger picks him up, reads the words carved on its side, "Put me back in the water. I am Paddle-to-the-Sea," and gently sends it back out into the world. One stranger, named Bill, gives Paddle-to-the-Sea much needed repairs, repaints him and adds a copper plate to the bottom, where he and all the other people along the way can etch details of where Paddle-to-the-Sea has been.

At the end of the story, years later, the young Indian boy, now a man, learns that his little boat is the subject of a newspaper story and has made a journey all the way to France. In the final scene, he is sitting in his own canoe:

> *In the canoe, the Indian smiled. Once he paused in a stroke, and rested his blade. For that instant he looked like his own*

---

[19] http://Awalkacrossmichigan.com/promote

Paddle. There was a song in his heart. It crept to his lips, but only the water and the wind could hear.

'You, Little Traveler! You made the journey, the Long Journey. You now know the things I have yet to know. You, Little Traveler! You were given a name, a true name in my father's lodge. Good Medicine, Little Traveler! You are truly a Paddle Person, a Paddle-to-the-Sea!'

This is my first book and, as I shove it off, like a little piece of twig into the torrent of words rushing headlong into the river of literature, I bid it farewell and wish it a joyous journey of adventure. Be strong, my little baby book. Watch out for the haters and bandersnatches. Make the Long Journey. Ride the raging rapids. Sail the bountiful seas to exotic ports of call. Return to me laden with stories and riches from your voyages.

Ok. I don't know about you, but that's about as maudlin as I can stand.

Like the little boy in *Paddle-to-the-Sea*, however, I would very much like to know where my little book wanderer has been to, so I created a special "**Booklog**," where I can track its journeys and you can follow the progress of it, too, if you want. I think it will be fun to watch. You can add your details and see the other places that *A Walk Across Michigan* has visited by signing the **Booklog (www.awalkacrossmichigan.com/booklog)**.

"What's next," you ask?

My answer is still the same: "I want it all!"

"I want to live the rest of my life deliberately. I want to do the important things; make valuable contributions that make a difference in the world and leave a legacy. I want adventure and excitement, enthusiasm and passion. I want to pursue that bucket list like a man with his hair on fire and wring the neck of each item on it like it was a Sunday dinner chicken. Ride the bull, or at least run with them. Grab for all the gusto I can get and then some."

Happy Trails & Endless Summer!
Will

P.S. One final thought for those who are considering retirement. I get asked quite often, "How do you like being retired?" As I write this, it's been a good eight months since I followed through on that. While I was exploring the whole idea, I talked to several other retired administrators and friends I knew and they all assured me that being retired was wonderful. No one said that they had retired too soon. Some said they wish they'd done it sooner. They went on and on about how great it was not to have to get up in the morning and go to work, not being tied to a schedule, being able to travel in the off seasons, and all the other benefits they were enjoying. Lies, LIES, **LIES!!** ---It's waaaaaay better than that! Just so you know.

If you'd like to keep tabs on me or connect, you can do so at:

http://WillSwartz.com

A Short History of the Shore-to-Shore Trail

Credit for the existence of the Michigan Shore-to-Shore Trail goes to a handful of early pioneers, who followed through on a shared vision to create a riding trail from one side of Michigan to the other. The names of the visionary trailblazers and their contributions are included in the *Michigan Trail Riders Guide Book* and expanded upon with more in-depth material in Rhoda Ritter's book, *Michigan Riding & Hiking Trail : True Stories of the First Crossing and Further Adventures.*

The STS grew from the efforts of a small group of people, that eventually became the early members of the Michigan Trail Riders Association (MTRA). They came up with the idea, following through with action by working with governmental organizations, blazing the trail, riding it and maintaining it. MTRA members have spent countless hours designing camps, participating in meetings and work bees, installing vault toilets, building bridges, improving trail sections, advocating with government agencies to develop policy, negotiating with private land owners, and more.

The earliest roots of the STS and the Trail Riders go back to the 1960's. Over a 30 year stretch of time, the trail grew from a vision to connect individual trails and paths on public and privately owned lands into the reality of a continuous, well-marked shore to shore riding and hiking trail. During that time the MTRA grew from a handful of enthusiastic horsemen and women to 1000+ members and has attracted members from a variety of states and other countries, including Canada, England and Germany. Many travel long distances to ride the trail in our state and to renew friendships and to make new ones as they return year after year.

The trail has a lot of history attached to it. At least 3 couples have been married on the trail. Several members have 50+ crossings and know the various sections as well as they know the streets in their cities. The current record holder for the most number of crossings is Rose Bos, who, as of the end of 2014, has crossed the state by horseback 78 times. Rose is 76 years young!

One of the hallmarks of the STS that is most appreciated by horsemen and women from around the world is the ability to ride the STS without the requirement of a guide or escort, proceeding through marvelous wooded stretches of Michigan's finest wilderness at their own pace. Camps designed for those with horse trailers and that are spaced a day's ride apart make the rides attractive to those who desire to experience a longer trip. Organized trail rides, with a trail boss and a bus to ferry riders back to their horses after they move their rigs in the morning to the ending point of their day's ride, are a feature that many riders highly appreciate.

One factor that made the STS Trail possible was the use of large tracts of State and National Forests across the middle of the state. These were already designated and in place as wilderness areas, set aside for all to enjoy without fear of development. In the early years, the STS was used by many different modes of transportation and the results were not always harmonious. As motorcycle companies began producing off road bikes and off road vehicles (ORVs) were developed, friction arose between the groups vying for use of the same spaces. Compromises were made by the different parties and policies were created that all could agree to. The STS Trail was designated as a hiker and horse only trail, while other trails have been set aside where horses are not allowed. So now, a system of well-groomed ORV trails criss-crosses the forest area and the STS crosses them too many times to count.

Today, a delicate balance exists that can be threatened whenever it faces the forces of inevitable change: land changes hands, politicians come and go, policies and laws are adopted, leadership changes in organizations with an interest in the Trail. Much of the land that the STS travels through is managed by the Department of Natural Resources and is subject to its oversight. An Equine Trailways Subcommittee advises and advocates for horseback riders, concerning trail use, camps and other policy matters.

The Michigan Trail Riders have given permission to include here their short history, contained in The Michigan Trail Rider's Guide Book for members.

> In the early 1960's, the idea of a horse trail going across Michigan, from Lake Michigan to Lake Huron, was conceived by horseback riders Fitch and Louise Williams, Tony and Sally Wilhelm, and Rex and Phyllis Garn, all of Grand Traverse County. The group visited Lost Creek Sky Ranch and the idea of riding across the state sparked a fire. Jim Hardy, owner of the dude ranch, worked on the east side of the trail. Jim's neighbor, Forest Rhodes, worked for the U.S. Forest Service. He helped Jim set up a network of trails from Tawas City to the Manistee River west of Frederick. The Traverse group worked on the west end of the trail. Fitch Williams helped

write a bill to establish such a trail and it was introduced in the Michigan Legislature by William Milliken, then a state senator. During this time (1962), Fred Haskins of the Department of Conservation (now the Department of Natural Resources) laid out the first section of the trail. It began south of Traverse City and extended 33 miles to Kalkaska. Volunteers from the Grand Traverse Saddle Club marked this first section of the trail with blue dots.

In 1963, Fitch Williams incorporated the Michigan Trail Riders Association and drew up the by-laws. From that point on, the work of many people made the entire trail a reality. Basil Smith of Kalkaska spearheaded efforts from Kalkaska to Island Lake. The Lions Club of Empire laid out and built the trail from Empire to Mud Lake. Jim Hardy of Luzerne worked with Forest Rhodes to complete the east end of the trail. Consumers Power Company allowed the trail to go through their property and even permitted some of the original camps to be on their land. Explorer Post 36, a Boy Scout group from Traverse City, played an important part in the original work on the trail. Jim Johnson of Empire let us use his land in town for a camp. Help came from every town along the trail and many individuals. In May, 1964, Governor Romney dedicated the trail at a ceremony in Kalkaska. An historical marker at the Kalkaska Camp commemorates the event.

Today, the Michigan Trail Riders Association continues to maintain and make improvements to both the trail and the camps, with regular work bees and funding various projects.

Each year, the Board of Directors choose sections of the trail for which they will be responsible. For an entire year they work to keep their section in good riding and hiking shape. Many volunteers assist those board members during projects and work bees, but they also work on their own to improve the trail, especially near their homes. The excellent state of the trail is a testament to their efforts and hard work.

My hope is that, as more riders and hikers discover the STS, it will become a rewarding legacy for those early visionaries who, literally, laid the groundwork for the trail so that future generations would have a means to explore our beautiful state.

I really must comment, at this point, that you rock! You have certainly surprised me with your determination by reading completely through this entire chapter. It's in an appendix at the back of the book and you even knew that a chapter, titled A Short History of the Shore-to-Shore Trail, could not possibly lead to a compelling and desperate romance between hopelessly flawed and miserable characters or to a mysterious encounter with a time traveling politician seeking reelection, and yet you still persevered. I'm impressed. You're the type of person who finishes what they start and every author would be thrilled to have you as a reader. I do have to inform you, sadly, that the book is done now. If you turn the pages, all you will see are the notes and citations pages, which really, even to me, are not that interesting!

Citations

Chapter One

"Antoine de Lamothe Cadillac." Encyclopedia of World Biography. 2004. Encyclopedia.com. (August 10, 2015). http://www.encyclopedia.com/doc/1G2-3404707126.html

"Encyclopedia Of Detroit." Cadillac, Antoine De La Mothe. Accessed August 10, 2015. http://detroithistorical.org/learn/encyclopedia-of-detroit/cadillac-antoine-de-la-mothe.

Irish, Brenda. "Battle for Wexford County! « Seeking Michigan." Seeking Michigan. November 27, 2012. Accessed August 10, 2015. http://seekingmichigan.org/look/2012/11/27/wexford-county-battle.

Smith, B. (2012, January 19). 6 Towns That Claim Paul Bunyan as Their Own (and What They Should Be Bragging About Instead). Retrieved August 10, 2015.

Chapter Seven

"A Brief History of Lumbering in Michigan." A Brief History of Lumbering in Michigan. Accessed August 10, 2015.

http://www.michigan-history.org/lumbering/LumberingBriefHistory.html.

Horton, O.W. (Photographer). 1876. Prize Winning Woodcarvers [Photograph]. Grand Rapids, #76, Stereo Card Collection, History & Special Collections Dept. Retrieved August 10, 2015 on the World Wide Web: http://www.furniturecityhistory.org/photo/965/prize-winning-wood-carvers.

Hotchkiss, George Woodward. "Saginaw Bay and Huron Shore : Tawas, Au Sable, Alpena, ETC. --Sketches of Lumbermen." In History of the Lumber and Forest Industry of the Northwest, 157. Chicago, Illinois: G.W. Hotchkiss &, 1898.

Loomis, Bill. "Shanty Boys, River Hogs and the Forests of Michigan." Shanty Boys, River Hogs and the Forests of Michigan. April 8, 2012. http://www.detroitnews.com/article/20120408/METRO/204080301#ixzz3fm7acxtB.

Schaetzl, Randall. "Big Wheels: A Michigan Innovation." Big Wheels. Accessed August 10, 2015. http://geo.msu.edu/extra/geogmich/big_wheels.html.

"Winfield Scott Gerrish." Winfield Scott Gerrish. Accessed August 10, 2015. http://www.migenweb.net/osceola/1884bios/gerrishw.html.

Chapter Eleven

Donovan, Jennifer. "Can We Bring the Grayling Back to Michigan?" Michigan Tech News. August 15, 2011. Accessed August 10, 2015. http://www.mtu.edu/news/stories/2011/august/can-bring-grayling-back-michigan.html.

Engle, Chris. "Resurrection: The Frankenstein Story of Michigan's Lost Fish." Petoskey News-Review. April 25, 2014. Accessed August 10, 2015. http://www.petoskeynews.com/gaylord/sports/outdoors/wild/

resurrection-the-frankenstein-story-of-michigan-s-lost-fish/article_a891ef62-cbf9-11e3-a7c8-0017a43b2370.html.

Tomelleri, Joseph R. "Michigan Grayling Only a Memory." Michigan.gov DNR. Accessed August 10, 2015. http://www.michigan.gov/dnr/0,4570,7-153-10364_18958-53612--,00.html.

Chapter Twelve

Etter, Dr. Dwayne, and Dr. Larry Visser. "Estimating Abundance of Black Bears in Michigan, Sifting Through the Sands of Time." Eastern Blackbear Workshop. Accessed August 10, 2015. http://www.easternblackbearworkshop.org/uploads/3/0/8/8/3088388/bear_population_estimation_in_mi_etter.pdf.

Flesher, John. "Girl, 12, Describes Frightening Bear Attack (with Video)." Freep.com. August 20, 2013. Accessed August 10, 2015. http://archive.freep.com/article/20130819/NEWS06/308190109/michigan-girl-12-jogging-bear-attack.

"Michigan Black Bear Facts." DNR Education and Outreach. November 19, 2004. Accessed August 10, 2015. http://www.michigan.gov/dnr/0,1607,7-153-10369-105034--,00.html.

Chapter Fifteen

Kane, Ethan. "Dendroica Kirtlandii Kirtland's Warbler." Animal Diversity Web. Accessed August 10, 2015. http://animaldiversity.org/accounts/dendroica_kirtlandii/.

"Kirtland's Warbler Breeding Range Conservation Plan." May 27, 2014. Accessed August 10, 2015. https://www.michigan.gov/documents/dnr/Kirtlands_Warbler_CP_457727_7.pdf.

"Kirtland's Warbler (Dendroica Kirtlandii)." Michigan Department of Natural Resources. Accessed August 10, 2015.

http://www.michigan.gov/dnr/0,4570,7-153-10370_12145_12202-32591--,00.html.

"Species Profile for Kirtland's Warbler (Setophaga Kirtlandii)." Species Profile for Kirtland's Warbler (Setophaga Kirtlandii). Accessed August 10, 2015. http://ecos.fws.gov/speciesProfile/profile/speciesProfile.action?spcode=B03I.

Chapter Sixteen

Cerveniak, Alex. "The Adams: History Revisited by Tom Deschaine." Hatches. April 19, 2010. Accessed August 11, 2015. http://hatchesmagazine.com/blogs/Hatches/2010/04/19/the-adams-history-revisited-by-tom-deschaine/.

"Island Still Moving." Record-Eagle, November 16, 1970.

Chapter Seventeen

Godfrey, Linda S., and Mark Sceurman. "Bizarre Beasts: Lake Leelanau Monster." In Weird Michigan: Your Travel Guide to Michigan's Local Legends and Best Kept Secrets, 90. New York, New York: Sterling Publishing, 2006.

Meyerson, Howard. "The Salmon Experiment: The Invention of a Lake Michigan Sport Fishery, and What Has Happened since." MLive. April 18, 2011. Accessed August 11, 2015. http://www.mlive.com/outdoors/index.ssf/2011/04/the_salmon_experiment_the_inve.html.

Morris, Christine. "Heritage CelebrationAnnual Event Pays Tribute to Leland and Fishtown - Grand Traverse Insider - Morning Star Publishing." Grand Traverse Insider. September 15, 2009. Accessed August 11, 2015. http://www.morningstarpublishing.com/articles/2009/09/15/grand_traverse_insider/news/leelanau_area/doc4aae9a600c0c1090710010.txt?viewmode=fullstory.

Sommers, Laurie Kay. Fishtown: Leland, Michigan's Historic Fishery. Arbutus Press, 2012.

Wolcott, Ilene. "Story behind the Leland Dam | Www.leelanaunews.com | Leelanau Enterprise." Leelanau Enterprise. Accessed August 11, 2015. http://www.leelanaunews.com/news/2012-06-21/Life_in_Leelanau/Story_behind_the_Leland_Dam.html.

Chapter Eighteen

Bingham, Emily. "The Ice Man Cutteth: Remembering Michigan's Forgotten Winter Harvest." Found Michigan. March 8, 2012. Accessed August 11, 2015. http://www.foundmichigan.org/wp/2012/03/08/ice-man-cutteth/.

Klein, Kristopher. "The Man Who Shipped New England Ice Around the World." History.com. August 29, 2012. Accessed August 11, 2015. http://www.history.com/news/the-man-who-shipped-new-england-ice-around-the-world.

Chapter Twenty

"Hop Industry Overview." USA Hops. Accessed August 11, 2015. http://www.usahops.org/index.cfm?fuseaction=hop_info&pageID=1.

Pagnotta, Chris. "20 Things You Didn't Know About Hops." Men's Journal. Accessed August 11, 2015.

INDEX

A

A Walk Across America xvii
A Walk in the Woods xvii
Acadia National Park 4
Adams fly 123
Alaska 105
alewives 76, 130, 131, 133
Allen, Tim 120
Ambrose, Stephen xviii
ants 66, 67
Appalachian Trail .... xviii, xix, 9, 57
Au Sable ... 2, 31, 32, 44, 50, 59, 64, 79, 96, 98, 170
AWOL on the Appalachian Trail xvii

B

Babe the Blue Ox 7
Battle of Manton 4, 6
beach. 8, 14, 24, 89, 131, 147, 148, 154
bears 4, 80, 86, 87, 88, 89, 113
beauty 32, 33, 50, 64, 73, 121, 144
beer 17, 120, 131, 148, 149, 150, 151
blisters 49, 50, 64
blueberry 2, 51, 52, 53
Boardman 2, 80, 114
Boston 138, 139
Bryson, Bill xvii
Bunyan, Paul 6, 7, 169

C

Cadillac 3, 4, 5, 6, 87, 169
Cadillackers 5, 108
California 6, 7, 28, 43
Calvin & Hobbes xxix
Camp Tapico 98, 102, 104
campground xii, 18, 24, 26, 27, 31, 33, 39, 59, 64, 80, 114, 123
camps 7, 14, 18, 33, 38, 43, 46, 50, 78, 102, 114, 163, 165, 166
Canada/Canadian 77, 104, 160, 164
canoe 55, 57, 77, 160
caribou 104
Carp River 129, 132
Cast Away xx
cherry 121
Clam Lake 3
coffee . 17, 117, 118, 119, 120, 123
Conway, Eustace xviii
Cooper, Alice xxvii
Crowley, Chris 153
Curtisville 7, 50

D

dam.. 50, 64, 79, 80, 123, 132, 133, 137
deer 37, 38, 51, 58, 105, 148
Department of Natural Resources . 32, 86, 87, 111, 126, 165, 166, 171
Detroit:
  City 3, 4, 16, 42, 77, 132, 169
  River 77

E

Empire ... xxiv, 7, 14, 15, 17, 18, 99, 129, 148, 152, 166

F

fishing .xviii, 28, 71, 73, 74, 75, 76, 77, 78, 79, 80, 95, 97, 98, 102, 103, 107, 108, 116, 123, 126, 127, 129, 130, 131, 132, 133, 137
Fishtown x, 97, 129, 130, 132, 133, 135, 137, 172
floating islands 124, 125, 126
Fort Michilimackinac 3
Fredric Tudor 138, 140

G

Gilbert, Elizabeth xix
gold .... xiii, 43, 56, 118
Goose Creek 98
Grand Rapids 46, 48, 170
Grass Lake 98, 102
Grayling 7, 32, 58, 64, 67, 78, 95, 96, 170, 171
Great Lakes . 76, 77, 134, 138, 154, 160

H

Hart Plaza 4
Havana.. 139
Henry David Thoreau ....xxv, 1, 21, 27, 31, 54, 71, 109, 135, 136, 147
Hiking Through xvii
hops................................148, 149, 150
Huron National Forest 2, 7, 8

I

ice ....x, 15, 45, 47, 101, 135, 136, 137, 138, 139, 173
ice houses........... 135, 137, 138, 139
Idaho 149
Isle Royale .... xviii, 57

J

Jenkins, Peter xvii
Joe's Friendly Tavern............. 14, 17

K

Kalkaska ....xx, 7, 61, 98, 99, 102, 104, 105, 109, 166
Kirtland's warbler....110, 111, 112
Kneff Lake 80, 96, 97
Kodiak x

L

Lakes:
   Dubonnet... 120, 123, 124, 125, 126, 143
   Garey 18, 144, 145, 148
   Guernsey...........................112, 113
   Huron ...xviii, 7, 23, 32, 96, 130, 155, 165
   Leelanau...... 130, 132, 137, 172
   St. Claire 77
   Superior 133, 154, 160
Last American Man xviii
Laumet, Antoine.............................3, 4
Leelanau Lake Monster 131
Leland.....x, 97, 129, 130, 132, 133, 134, 137, 172, 173
Lewis and Clark............................ xviii
librarians......................x, 90, 91, 126
logging wheels 46
Lost Lake Pathway....................... 143
Louis XIV, King 4
Louisiana, Governor of....................4
Lower Peninsula 2, 86
lumber....16, 32, 42, 43, 45, 46, 47, 48, 78, 79, 132, 133, 138
Lumberman's Monument.... 36, 39
Luzerne.................................7, 64, 166
Lyme disease.................................... 58

M

Mackinac:
    Bridge xviii
    City ....xviii, 4
Maine 4, 6, 41
Manistee 2, 39, 47, 80, 165
Manitou:
    Island 97
    Lake 97
Manton 5, 6
Mantonites 5
Mayhem Swamp 104, 105, 106, 107
McKinley 7, 19, 50, 61
mice 103
Michigan:
    Association for Media in Education x
    Brewer's Guild 149
    Department of Tourism 120
    Michigan History Magazine 5
    Lake . xviii, 7, 14, 23, 28, 32, 46, 49, 84, 97, 121, 123, 129, 130, 133, 137, 143, 148, 154, 155, 165, 172
Michigan Shore-to-Shore Riding and Hiking Trail .... *See* STS
Miller, David xvii
Minnesota 6
Mio 7, 32, 64
mosquitoes 58, 105
Mount Cadillac 4
Mountain and Blues Festival 7
Mud Lake .... *See* Lake Dubonnet

mushrooms 52, 65, 73

N

National Cherry Festival 122
North Country Trail .... xx, 2

O

off road 165
Ontario 110
Oregon 149
Oscoda .. 6, 7, 19, 23, 32, 44, 64, 98
Oscoda Press 6
Ottawa 129

P

Pacific Coast Trail 9
Pacific Crest Trail xix
Platte River 123, 131

R

rain 65, 109
retirement ...... xxix, 33, 70, 80, 162
Retirement xxviii
River Road Horse Camp 36
Rose Bos 164

S

salmon 130, 131, 133, 172
Scouts 57, 102, 103

Short's Local's American Lager 151
Sleeping Bear Dunes 7, 17
South Branch 7, 39, 50
South Branch Horse Camp 36
St. Lawrence River 160
Strayed, Cheryl xvii
STS .xix, xx, xxi, 3, 6, 7, 8, 9, 10, 11, 23, 24, 25, 33, 40, 51, 67, 70, 77, 79, 85, 87, 88, 95, 102, 106, 110, 114, 123, 129, 143, 147, 163, 164, 165, 167
Stutzman, Paul xvii

T

ticks 57, 58, 59
Toledo 132
Trail Riders ix, 9, 18, 87, 163, 164, 165, 166
Traverse City 7, 16, 121, 122, 123, 125, 149, 166

trout 28, 32, 76, 79, 80, 81, 121, 130

U

U.S. Forest Service 165
Undaunted Courage xviii
Upper Peninsula 77, 86, 90

W

Washington 149
Wexford county 4, 5, 6, 169
Wild xvii
wilderness .... xii, xiv, 9, 13, 14, 72, 84, 85, 112, 113, 116, 164
Wisconsin 90, 91, 92, 110

Y

Yakima Valley 149